MORE DASH THAN CASH

VOGUE

MORE DASH THAN CASH

LINDA WATSON
ROSIE MARTIN

BCA
LONDON · NEW YORK · SYDNEY · TORONTO

This edition published 1992 by BCA by arrangement with The Condé Nast
Publications Ltd. an imprint of Random House UK Ltd.

CN6389
Designed by Write Image Ltd

Picture Research by Shona Wood

Set in Times and Eurostyle by SX Composing Ltd
Origination by Colorlito, Milan
Printed and bound in Italy by Graphicom

A catalogue record for this book is available from the British Library.

CONTENTS

INTRODUCTION 7

HOT OFF THE PRESS 9

SHOPPING LOGIC 51

WHAT MAKES A GREAT GARMENT? 75

THE CLASSICS 91

GROOMING 129

INTRODUCTION

There is much more to looking good than a weighty wallet. The most expensive labels in the world are an unconvincing veneer if they fight with your lifestyle, drown your personality and turn you into a fashion clone. A winning appearance requires imagination, but never loses sight of practicalities. Today, a limited budget is a lame excuse for not making the effort. Women now, more than ever, have the run of a wide field of choices. As High Street stores multiply, they compete for our attention by interpreting high fashion and using their ingenuity to explore new territory. It's up to you to pick out the best.

This book is not a directory—it won't point the finger at clothes you should rush out and buy, nor will it tell you *what* to wear *when*. Its aim is to untangle the web, hand you the ammunition—the knowledge—so you can tell at a glance what will last or fall apart, what you'll wear and wear and what's doomed to be a one-season wonder. Fashion is a roller-coaster ride of changes, but some rules last for ever. The right height of heel will always update proportions, for example; good grooming is a constant prerequisite; quality is eternal; certain shapes will maximise your figure type, others will kill it dead.

Outdated concepts may have to fall by the wayside. Extracting maximum mileage from a limited number of clothes means viewing them with an unbiased eye. Be ready to rethink your approach towards colour, to look at pieces from a fresh angle, to merge new ideas with your taste level. The key is to understand when it's worth spending more. If you develop a well-planned, non-obsessive strategy, dressing well becomes second nature.

Great clothes are unobtrusive, but have the power to make a world of difference. The boost to your confidence is uncalculable—you exude enthusiasm, even make it clear you're on the ball. *More Dash Than Cash* demystifies fashion, takes you through your paces and allows you to take control. Enjoy it, you're in the driving seat.

HOT OFF THE PRESS

A quiet word in the ear of sloppy dressers: fashion *is* important. You ask why? Basically, nothing speaks louder about your state of mind than clothes, hair and make-up that are out of sync with the times. Ex-students who, years after the last exam, still live in shabby sweaters and floppy jeans are sending out signals that say they're not ready to go forward on their own; sticking with a hairstyle and make-up format that are relics of a confidence peak warns that a woman has reached a plateau where ambitions can get pushed to one side. If you're not on top of the latest looks, chances are you've switched off from the rest of the world—the current issues, its key players: 'Fashion is like a television screen on the world,' says designer Christian Lacroix, 'made up of all the present trends—music, painting, news, etc.' The trick is knowing how to keep it switched on.

Left *You wouldn't wear it to the office – but you can pick up on the skirt length, the weight of the shoes and rush out to buy a gingham skirt.*

Being fashionable isn't difficult. You don't have to be extreme or copy every runway shenanigan that makes headlines in fashion capitals. Only fashion victims lift whole looks from a designer's cutting table and indiscriminately pile on fashionable labels. These are the markings of a woman who lacks confidence, let alone imagination. Clothes are a way of defining yourself rather than a mechanism to push you into the mainstream. A far more intelligent approach is to pursue a personal sense of style that includes fashion elements; that means knowing about the big stories and the details—the silhouette, proportions, fabrics, colours, accessories, when to change your hair or height of shoe—and linking them to a basic working wardrobe in ways all your own.

Style bears the hallmarks of your personality. It's a timeless, constant quality that draws you to a way of dressing you feel comfortable with. Some people are born with instinctive good style: they share a common ground in not being overdressed, and are not just clothes hangers for outrageous fashions, but have a special, unforced identity with which they are obviously at ease. The trick is knowing what is right for you. Clothes you battle with and that make you self-conscious destroy any hope of style. 'You should wear your clothes, not let the clothes wear you,' warns British designer Betty Jackson. Good style is not something you can copy—clothes that you admire on someone else won't necessarily be a success for you—but it can be developed with practice, a will to experiment and an honest assessment of your personality and way of life. Think long and hard about how you want to be perceived, your lifestyle and to a lesser extent your shape and age. How you mix colours and textures, the extent you accessorise, the complexity or simplicity of the complete look, personal items—maybe pieces of antique clothing, hats, ethnic jewellery or fabric you've bought abroad—will stamp your distinguishing marks and if you don't see them on anyone else that's good news, not a reason to think they're not *de rigueur*. Step out of the mould: going with the flow like everyone else is safe but mediocre, and witness the boost to your self-esteem.

Originality means constantly viewing clothes from a new angle. This is why fashion with its perpetual motion, its novelty, fun and rejection of anything ordinary, is such a potent, educative medium. Sometimes its movements are lit up in lights, often it works in more subtle ways. For instance, you may have picked up on the new length of skirt, but are you clear what can make it look really new—the right jacket, fabrics, colours, attitude and occasion? The emphasis is on being well informed.

'If a woman is poorly dressed you notice the clothes. If she is impeccably dressed, you notice the woman.'

COCO CHANEL

NOT JUST PRETTY PICTURES

Nobody said an inspired appearance wouldn't require effort.
Although a limited budget in no way precludes you from looking
good—as this book will illustrate—it does impose three necessi-
ties: motivation, knowledge and innovation. The medium that
ignitcs all these is a quality, glossy fashion magazine. By bringing
together the best photographers, models, locations, writers,
editors and designers, a good magazine creates such a glamorous
visual image the reader starts to dream. It's that dreaming that
sets you thinking, gets you excited about fashion so you treat it as
a subject worth working on.

Communicating information is a magazine's *raison d'être*.
Although your bank balance may stop you filling your wardrobe
with the expensive labels you see in its pages, an understanding
of fashion must start with a publication that deals predominantly
with the most influential designers. The trouble with magazines
that report only mass-market fashion is that you're really seeing
diluted versions of ideas that the designer giants came up with
anything up to a year previously.

Above *Fashion photography knocks
you off balance so you're ready to
accept something new. The
accessories are unwearable, the
clothes are not central to the
picture, but the reader can be
inspired by a romantic theme that
role plays with medievalism,
principal-boy swagger and huntress
jackets and boots.*

Designers at the top end of fashion are there for a reason—
their ability to invent—and it is their concepts that eventually
trickle down to the High Street. Magazines at the cutting edge of
fashion are privy to the ready-to-wear collections in Milan, Paris,
London and New York, which occur in March (the next autumn/
winter clothes) and October (spring/summer), and in *Vogue*'s
case are reported usually in the August and February issues re-
spectively. Even if you are not a regular magazine buff, these are
the issues most worth investing in, so you learn about designs
several months before they appear in the shops. The difficulty is
drumming up enough enthusiasm for, say, winter clothes in
August when they hit the news stands, but it's important to 'get
an eye in' ahead of time because knowing what's coming in
winter will influence what you buy for summer. Plus, you're in a
position to use some of the details, themes and colours early; if
you wait till fashion trends hit the High Street, as far as fashion
experts are concerned, they are already out of date.

On the surface, the haute couture collections that *Vogue*
records in April and October may have little relevance to your
wardrobe at home. The prices involved are huge and middle-
market labels can never hope to mirror the couturier's lavish
beading, time-consuming intricacies and cutting expertise. However, traditionally, it is inside the cloistered buildings of haute
couture houses that designers are pushed to their creative limits,
unbridled by factors that constrict them in ready-to-wear, such as
wearability, fabrics, time and cost. Here the seeds of many
fashion trends are sown, which filter down through the ready-to-
wear and ultimately into cheaper brands. In recent seasons, a
natural raffia/straw/wicker element threaded through haute couture, which was easily interpreted with very little expense. How
wonderful to be handed the chance to lead the way.

The sheer volume of images streaming out from the runways
can be confusing, but a good magazine editor will edit them into
coherent trends and sift out the gimmicks, leaving only the direc-
tional fashion. Throughout the season, the magazine's intention
is to offer variables, showing how the runways can be worked to
their maximum potential. The advantage fashion editors have is
that they see the whole fashion market—from the established,
respected names to the newest designer with the first flickers of
talent. You should see the flurry of activity in the fashion room at
Vogue: rails upon rails of clothes, with fashion editors and their
assistants experimenting with accessories, mixing labels, trying
on clothes to assess the way they hang, deciphering which are the
most perfectly shaped trousers, coats, shirts, etc.

HIGH FASHION TO HIGH STREET: HOW IT WORKS

Between *Vogue* running the photograph on the left and the other two, there are thirteen months—the time it takes for fashion to travel from runway to High Street. (left) This look, which draws inspiration from the life and times of Forties gangsters Bonnie and Clyde, was an innovative image, not just because of the getaway car and mock sub-machine gun, but because of the John Galliano suit. It was new for two reasons: firstly, mannish pinstripes were being worn by a woman; secondly, the skirt was long and had a split that revealed a good deal of leg. The tough sexiness of a moll provided the mood. Just over a year later the look hit the High Street. It was simpler, less theatrical, but picked up on the mood and core elements of the original and presented them in a wearable form: (centre) a pinstripe shorts suit; (right) an ankle-length skirt that shows the leg, topped with a man's jacket; both worn with that heavy dose of sex appeal.

This process is akin to concentrated shopping and saves the reader time by handing her the best shapes and colours on a plate. The pieces that pass the test are hurriedly packed into bulging suitcases and taken to be photographed. On the shoot, the editor starts to improvise: tying a shirt in a new way; using a scarf or piece of antique fabric as a skirt; juxtaposing colours to create a surprise; mixing evening accessories with day wear. One fashion editor is infamous for telling a model to slip her legs through the arms of a cardigan and wear it as a pair of trousers. Magazines teach you to adjust your ideas of what's appropriate: 'If you see a shot of a denim shirt worn with a ballroom skirt, don't say how ridiculous; think if denim can penetrate even evening wear, it's clearly an important thread through the collections,' advises Harrods's fashion consultant, Vanessa de Lisle. The photographer, editor, hair and make-up artist have a theme in mind and are interpreting it in the most original evocative way they know. 'Give 'em [the readers] what they never knew they wanted!' was the brief American *Vogue*'s great former editor, Diana Vreeland, once gave her fashion editors: if the magazine's doing its job well you won't see what you expect to find.

Open its pages with an open mind—don't dismiss obscure pictures out of hand—look at extremes and try to understand them. The swashbuckling fencer on page 125, wearing slicked hair, an eye patch, a steely glare, bustier, tight leggings, silver beads and buckled shoes is a role model that would no doubt be viewed with some scepticism if imitated at the office, but no matter: *Vogue* isn't dictating, it's telling you about fashion's new moods, colours and points of emphasis. In the case of the fencer, she is an icon for fashion's one-time preoccupation with body-conscious clothes, metallics and cavalier flamboyancy, but how you adapt these ideas—not necessarily the actual clothes—is left to you. The purpose of the photograph is to nudge you off balance, knock you out of a groove, so you're ready to accept change, and sometimes the only image that does the job is a strong one.

WHERE READERS GO WRONG

Whilst magazine glossies are powerful vehicles for escapism, dreams have to be kept in check. It's no good going into a trance about sunny distant shores, the glamorous lifestyles of the rich and famous, the long-legged figures of models in perfect clothes, and ending up feeling dissatisfied with your lot. Chances are then you'll throw the magazine away, frustrated that it never shows clothes you can afford and fashion becomes a dirty word for good. Keep your feet on the ground and remember that if magazines do show some clothes whose prices seem inexplicably high, it's not through any malicious intention to torment the reader, but because the best fashion features are usually found in expensive lines. No one is asking you to rush out and buy all the clothes in fashion pages; magazines serve to show fashion's direction, they are never intended to be just catalogues. Even if the prices *were* lower, you can't lift a whole look from a page and put it on yourself. Firstly, you are probably physically different from the model in proportions and colouring. Secondly, your environment is not the same. Thirdly, you shouldn't be emulating others—you should be the person they turn to for inspiration!

HOW YOU SHOULD USE A MAGAZINE

Absorbing fashion is like osmosis: it comes gradually to anyone who's willing to let it in. The more images you see, the more quickly you'll become sensitive to its nuances.

• Dissect the fashion pages with a toothcomb. Circle what you like, cut pages out, even compile a scrapbook.

• Points to look for: proportions, themes, colours, fabrics and accessories. It is fashion's intrinsic peculiarity that designers work independently of one another, yet more times than not are united in their directions for the season. New themes may carry the distinguishing marks of each designer, but amongst the trees you can see the common wood. Work out whether the dominant shape is essentially narrow, like a vertical line, or marks out an upright inverted triangle. Is the weight on top or below, or is it evenly distributed? Have the designers looked to a common source for inspiration? Is the source something you could expand on? If the shapes are similar to those of previous seasons, try to distinguish what has been changed to make the look new.

• Questions to ask yourself: Where is the focus? Is the waist accentuated? What length is the skirt? How long is the jacket? Where does it cut the skirt? Are the legs a feature? Is the bust important? How high and heavy are the heels? Why, when fashion editors have so much to choose from, have they selected that particular jacket or skirt? What does it have in common with the rest of the pieces in the story? What is the hair doing? Has the make-up changed?

• Look beyond the main stories to the subtleties. For example, a simple slip dress might come through strongly but the precise scoop of its neckline could make the difference between one that makes it and one that just misses.

• Pick up a mood from a fashion story. Even when the clothes are not shown as clearly as you would wish, look at the lighting, the location, the attitude of the model—is it film-star glamour, energetic or feminine? The clothes may be expensive, but a mood can be created on any budget with make-up, the right fabrics and colours. A photograph is not a haphazard affair, it's designed to tell the reader as much as possible. For example, black-and-white film may indicate when important shapes, not colours, are being introduced. A Chanel jacket and jeans worn by model Claudia Schiffer on a beach in the Caribbean may seem a long way from the reality of most people's lives, but from it we can learn that: (a) beach wear may be more elegant if you're covered up; (b) a structured jacket can be made to look casual.

● Look for basic items that reappear season after season, such as blazers, classic trousers, white shirts, bodies and leggings.

● Don't just look at the pictures; read the text, captions and headings, which will spell out points you may have missed. It's not unusual for fashion to reflect the way women are feeling about themselves at a given time—their priorities, their needs, their hopes and their frustrations. Copy writers make it their job to extract new attitudes and choose their words carefully.

OTHER POINTS OF REFERENCE

All good newspapers have a regular fashion column. They're great for immediate reports from the runways, and often run extra fashion pages during the collections. Outside the collections, though, frantic deadlines and newspaper reproduction can cramp their style visually. The advantage of newspapers is that their journalists usually write about the current season, which will jog your memory about what you discovered in magazines.

Foreign glossies also make for good reference material, especially some French, Italian and American ones. The stockists, of course, will have little relevance, but the extra images can only heighten your awareness of the season's mood. Plus, they prove that the silhouettes and moods you've already spotted can be interpreted by a different selection of clothes, which is a lesson you can apply to your own wardrobe. Flicking through back copies of magazines also has worth, because out-dated concepts stand out a mile. You'll find true classic elements don't actually change too much, but the way they're styled may have undergone a total transformation: it is instructive to compare the length of skirt showing below a blazer, the different heights of shoes, the hair, the location and accessories.

Pay designer shops a visit to see how an item you've seen in a magazine actually looks on the hanger. Feel it, really get to grips with the type of fabric, cut and subtle details you'll be looking for. Try it on to see if it's going to be a look that's suitable for you and judge how it would work with your existing clothes. The silence and the clothes hanging up like prize exhibits can make designer shops seem intimidating, but you're entitled to look round with no obligation to buy. If you really can't face them, a morning spent window shopping is the next best thing.

Now set yourself a test: notice what other people wear—in the street, at parties, on television. Ask yourself why you love or dislike what they have on and make a mental note of how you would change things.

Right The elegance of tall slender Egyptian columns underlines the mood of a statuesque dress.

WHAT A DIFFERENCE A YEAR MAKES

Compare Chanel from one year to the next. Forget the price tags for the moment—note the changes in proportion and detail.

Above left

The jacket: over the bottom, fitted, with a curvaceous zip fastening, tweed

The skirt: narrow, eight inches above the knee, stretch denim, cut in half by jacket

Shoes: pretty pumps, flat

Accessories: pearl ropes, gilt, lots of it, the hips are made a fuss of; gloves

Top layer: denim jacket

Basics: a white T-shirt

Emphasis: on the jacket and legs

Above right

The jacket: still tweed but has shrunk to waist level, more boxy, no fastening

The skirt: calf-length, narrow,

weighty fabric, uncovered by jacket

Shoes: heavy-look platform boots

Accessories: still chunky, but this time the waist is the body part played up

Top layer: a wool stole

Basics: a black skinny crewneck

Emphasis: on the new length of skirt, an elongated lean look

FROM RUNWAY TO MAGAZINE TO PRACTICALITIES: THE THREE STAGES OF FEATHERS

There's something to be learnt from even the most unwearable clothes. **Left** Thierry Mugler's showgirl plumes on a jacket and boots, sashaying down the runway, made for a spectacle—but who has the nerve to wear them? **Centre** *Vogue* picked up on the theme and reported the same frou frou mood, but wearability was still in question. **Right** Then came the solution of how to add a fashion feature to a wardrobe unobtrusively and without a heavy financial outlay—a dainty bag of down with a cheeky streak that nods to the Mugler original.

PUTTING IT INTO PRACTICE

If you've done your homework, you'll know how to adapt your existing wardrobe to make it look up to the minute, by, say, adjusting proportions, copying the key accessories, mixing fabrics in a novel way, perking up an old jacket with the most modern-shaped trousers, tracking down a fashion colour, re-working your make-up and hair. You'll also be ready for the trends that travel from runway to the cheaper market, which will happen over the following seasons, and be first to pick out key pieces that bear out dominant themes. With practice, you'll learn to recognise a knock-off Giorgio Armani trouser suit or Azzedine Alaïa body, or a particularly well-shaped, anonymous piece that summarises the feeling all the designers were putting across—a crisp shirt *tied* in the right way, a supremely *elegant* dress, a *cossetting romantic* coat. Pursue a new shape, but cut costs by buying it in a cheaper fabric—a good tweed where the top designers were using suede or leather, cotton where they

worked with silk. More accessible ranges may have a policy of using half- instead of full-lining, perhaps producing 'mohair' that isn't but looks like it, or mixing cashmere with a little wool and nylon, but the shape and accessories—if not always the fit—can admirably echo the high-fashion lines. Of course, some cheaper-range labels have their own finger on the pulse. Says Monica Zipper of Monix: 'I've produced cashmere trenches at the same time as Arabella Pollen and Karl Lagerfeld.' If you have done your research well, you'll be quick to recognise their worth.

What's so wonderful now is that every woman is free to mould fashion into whatever shape she chooses. Time was, women used to carry round a label: 'She's a career woman; she's bohemian; she's a mother,' people would say narrowly. Mercifully, such sweeping judgments are irrelevant now because a woman can be many different things. 'Clothes are a great advantage women have over men,' believes fashion journalist Sarah Mower. 'They can say we're efficient, clever, personally going places, and then at night play up our romantic, sexual, creative sides—be whatever we want them to be.' Nan Kempner, one of New York's purveyors of good taste, agrees: 'A woman dresses for her morale. Being well-dressed is like Linus's protective blanket in *Charlie Brown*. You have to get dressed every day, so why not make it amusing? For instance, I like to play roles in different outfits—it's great guessing who I am for the day!' Which only goes to show that clothes are a source of fun, but also are open invitations to understanding our character and mood, and interpreting what's in magazines into something that suits both of these is the best fashion of all.

Left *Designer fashion can be strikingly simple.*

WARDROBE TACTICS

The best wardrobe is one taken seriously. Yes, you can have fun with clothes, but they won't be versatile and stylish without forethought, organisation and care. Treat them to the attention you'd pay a room you want to decorate: think how you'd patch-test paint on the wall, pin fabric swatches on a sofa, and stretch and pull them to see how they'd wear. Why should what you wear be different? The goal is that the moment you open the cupboard doors, and flick through the rails, you should see plenty to suit your mood. The start means rewinding back to basics, to uncomplicated foundation pieces that guarantee wearability, on top of which are layered your trade-marks—accessories, colours and styling. You may have to explode many of the conventions you feel comfortable with, even take a walk on the wild side, but the reward for your efforts is infinite variety.

Left *Nothing to wear . . .*

SPACE CRAFT

It's imperative to have a good place to keep your clothes. Slinging them over a chair to collect dust and crumple is not only slovenly but makes dressing haphazard. How can you expect to have style if how you look depends on what's top of the pile? A wardrobe should be no idle consideration: it should be as much of a pleasure as any other piece of furniture at home. Treasure it, buy it presents, really make it an issue. That way, you'll relish time spent in its company and be encouraged to experiment with its contents. The most glamorous is an antique gentleman's wardrobe in a rich dark wood with tiny drawers and compartments that make organisation easy. You can strike lucky at antique markets and in auction salerooms, especially in the country, though the very best may be disguised under thick layers of paint. A well designed wardrobe is one tall enough to take dresses *and* knee-high boots without squashing either; it has full-length mirrors on both doors so you can scrutinise your front and back, and is well lit, preferably with daylight, so colours look true. Sliding doors are a problem—they make access to the wardrobe's centre difficult. Unless you're fortunate enough to have a walk-in wardrobe, front-to-back rails hold less than ones that run widthways, and also make seeing what you have more difficult; two rails on the other hand, one above the other, are especially useful if you have lots of short skirts, shirts and jackets. What's critical is that clothes are nowhere near damp walls, well-circulated with air and far from food smells—so think twice about placing a wardrobe directly above a kitchen.

In an ideal world, you'd have space between hangers, lots of shelves, and drawers deep enough not to click sweaters; the reality can seem cramped but a well-organised wardrobe is a bigger one. It's vital not to waste space between the bottom of hanging clothes and the wardrobe's base, and you can maximise that by buying shallow hangers; some modern plastic ones are unnecessary giants. Work out whether you could fit in an extra low shelf about six inches from the bottom to double the area for shoes. Shelves are often more useful than drawers because you can see at a glance what you have. Stackable wire baskets, box files, office trays and shoe boxes will fill in precious gaps and marshal socks, underwear and T-shirts. For long clothes, which restrict use of the wardrobe's floor, use double-layer—or more—hangers, so you economise widthways. Tidy-bags, which consist of rows of pockets, hung on the back of the wardrobe door can cope with all the bits and pieces you can never find.

It's worth picking the brains of imaginative, modern furniture stores that make space-saving their business, but don't be afraid to deploy everyday items to deal with problems of overspill. Hat boxes—antique ones have most character—look great towered in the corner of a room and can contain anything from leggings to accessories. Wooden wine racks serve a dual purpose by being almost tailor-made for shoes. Tin tuck boxes and trunks—the sort children take to boarding school—can be dug out of junk shops or the loft, covered with fabric and turned into keep safes for sweaters. Simple aluminium-framed canvas wardrobes that zip up and look like stripey beach huts will separate out coats and evening dresses you hardly ever wear but which eat up room, and bric-à-brac markets are popular graveyards for freestanding clothes rails discarded by retailers. Old dark wooden ones are the most covetable and, once concealed behind a striped screen or maybe white muslin drapes, they can turn into a self-contained dressing-room. Most women, though, shouldn't need such excessive amounts of space, and if they could fill more they can be justifiably accused of hoarding and the advice is—take stock!

EDITING DOWN

A wardrobe only works if everything is worn and nothing is kept for sentimental reasons. Hanging on to dross can colour what you think of the rest of your clothes. Pruning out the dead wood will let the good clothes be seen so they influence what you buy next, and choosing what to wear each morning becomes less confusing. Put aside a day and pull everything out of your wardrobe and throw it on to the bed. Next, spring clean inside—wash and paint it. Then try everything on and make three piles: the first for things you're discarding, the second for clothes that need repairing, the third for ones you will keep.

Never throw anything you decide to abandon into the dustbin. Charity shops are always crying out for clothes and at the very least you could offer them to friends, maybe even do a swap. Sewing on buttons, rectifying dropped hems, taking the rubbed wool off sweaters with tape, bridging the backs of holes with iron-on invisible adhesive web, polishing shoes, keeping them well-heeled, and so on, are the finer points of good grooming. Try to devote an evening once a month to catch up on the repair jobs that only get worse if left. Go to work on stains: treat chocolate with glycerine and rinse with warm soapy water; dab lipstick with eucalyptus oil and wash in hot water and soap; dissolve aspirins in the washing water to remove perspiration marks.

LETTING GO

Hold on to clothes that:

- make you feel good or you're complimented on
- fit well
- are timeless, good quality classics
- contain shapes and features you recognise from current magazines

Discard anything that:

- you never wear
- is ill-fitting, unflattering
- is past its sell-by date, like washed-up sweaters and T-shirts, misshapen shoes
- you've bought good replacements for
- shouldn't be there—remember wardrobes are for clothes only, not for forgetting about things you don't know what to do with

Right *If you're organised, looking great is as simple as black and white.*

WHAT MAKES A GREAT WARDROBE

Versatility is the key word, which means having clothes that cope with every situation, so you don't have to rush out to buy something new the minute an invitation drops through the letterbox. The aim is to extract the maximum of looks from the minimum of clothes with the least possible effort and expense. A clever wardrobe:

● has limitless permutations

● will accommodate all the new clothes you do buy

● can be worn even when fashion changes.

To save time and make ringing the changes easier, the clothes you want to keep have to be ordered well. The big mistake is to hang them together as 'outfits' or in bands of colour. Instead, block all your shirts together and separate them from blocks of jackets and trousers, etc. Within each block, graduate colour but keep stripes together and patterns together. Put the heaviest group—jackets—at one end of a rail and work through jeans, wool trousers and skirts, to the lightest—probably silk shirts. Sweaters, however, will stretch if hung, and are best laid flat unfolded; otherwise, fold them horizontally with just the arms—not the shoulders—tucked under to create less bulk; never fold them lengthways because the crease takes ages to drop out. Although newly ironed shirts are better put on hangers, if room is very scarce, shirts folded and laid on a shelf will emerge less squashed. More shoes can be stored if they stay in their boxes, which must be labelled so you don't have to open them all to pinpoint the right pair. The trick is to cut down the sides of the boxes at one end, so you can bend the end back and slide out the shoes without disrupting the pile. Belts should be hung, not rolled, so they don't crack. It's best to keep bags on a shelf—not hung up or thrown on the floor where they'll get dusty. Fold rather than roll tights so they don't over stretch, and put them in a drawer beside your underwear. Scarves should be folded on a shelf, or laid over a trouser hanger, but never just thrown over a hook. Keep costume jewellery where you can see what you have, not jumbled together so it chips. Don't mix pearls with gilt jewellery because the pearls soon scratch and look dull. Long beads are less likely to tangle if hung, but heavy strings should be wound into a spiral on a flat surface to avoid tensions and breakages. Glass desk-tidiers make efficient compartmentalisers for accessories and scouring office suppliers and stationers will expose Perspex miniature drawer systems and tiny boxes.

CLOTHES SWAP

The biggest restraint you can put on your clothes is to separate them into categories. Summer, winter, evening, day, work, home, holiday are all compartments we tend to slot our life into, but our wardrobe doesn't have to follow suit. Traditional dress codes have started to break down: society is less structured than ever before, to the extent that even rock 'n' royalty rub shoulders; women who work may not have time to rush home and change before going out, and many people today work from home. Clothes have to play more than one role.

That's good news for anyone balancing finances: a simple white shirt, for example, can be worn with jeans and a pretty shoe during the day, with fine fabrics and glamorous jewellery for evening, over a T-shirt or poloneck in the winter, and tied into a knot at the waist in summer. The beauty is, any one of the above ways of wearing it could be interchanged with any of the occasions. The freedom is yours.

The common denominator of this crossover principle is surprise, questioning all the rules that used to apply, wearing pieces you wouldn't expect to be compatible or suit an occasion. Cultivate a creative attitude, and you're on the road to developing a personal style. Fashion doesn't stop with the designer, but lays itself open to be interpreted any way you like, provided you approach it with confidence.

Seasonless dressing

The key here is to work with layers. A body under a shirt, with a cardigan and lightweight wool jacket over the top looks great for winter, but can also form the bare bones of a summer outfit: just remove one or two elements, it doesn't matter which. Tunics, leggings and jeans easily cross the season's boundaries: tunics run the course with slim trousers, through leggings to cotton shorts, and can even be worn with bare legs; leggings work equally well with a tailored jacket, a warm sloppy Joe or a cool shirt; and jeans are infamous for going with just about everything. Try to buy fabrics not restricted to a few months of the year, which means bypassing extremes. Anything heavy, thick, or incredibly fine is less useful than light wool, cotton, suede, denim, crepe, even silk. Colour sense means rejecting roles that limit pale to summer and dark to winter. With the right shoes and layers, any spectrum looks right—use cream and pastels to brighten up a cloudy day and, say, navy to sharpen up loose summery clothes.

Crossing time zones

The am/pm crossover holds a wealth of possibilities of what can be worn with what—and when. A lustrous beaded jacket with narrow pants and pretty mules is appropriate during the evening, but equally it's now a look for nine to five. Similarly, a daytime denim shirt or biker jacket worn with taffeta or satin sweeping skirts can find its way into the ballroom, and make the statement that too formal for evening looks frumpy.

The rich materials that were once the prerogative of after dark now don't look too dressy in daylight: brocade, organza and

'So long as something is beautiful, it doesn't matter when you wear it.'

LUCINDA CHAMBERS

FASHION DIRECTOR,

BRITISH *VOGUE*

Left and above *Crossing time zones: a beaded jacket with jeans can day-trip, but equally it's a look for evening. Gianni Versace shows how even denim can now be invited to the ball.*

Right *Urban
tweed: city
dressing can
take a lead from
its country
cousins.*

velvet, say, on a tunic or shirt, can all brighten work hours if mixed with tougher elements, such as a structured jacket or well-cut trousers. Satin often sees the light via a tiny bag, as bright and as delicious as a fruit drop.

Country comes to town
Although this doesn't extend as far as wearing Barbours in Bond Street, the tweeds and more relaxed, long knits, previously the preserve of a weekend break, are now relevant in the city. When Karl Lagerfeld threaded the tweed on Chanel's signature jackets with glittering silver thread and raffia, not only was he endorsing tweed as a thoroughly modern fabric, he was also telling the city suit to ease up, have some fun. Fierce power dressing is a thing of the past, and it's possible to address the boardroom in something less structured, more individual. Let the imagination run to mariners' blazers, safari jackets, riding boots, jodhpurs.

The ladies' man
Nothing looks sexier on a woman than mannish pinstripes, men's jackets, trousers, vests, shirts and even cuff links. Men's wear crosses genders and we love it for its simplicity and classic good looks. Think Lauren Bacall and Marlene Dietrich.

Underwear as outerwear
This turnabout first showed its face at the end of the Eighties in the form of a bra, heavily disguised with spangles and tassels, and discreetly hidden in the darkness of night clubs in London. Then, lingerie suddenly threw out its inhibitions, and with all its lace, silk, sensuality and bareness stepped into the daylight. French haute couture designers created satin dresses that bore the markings of petticoats, and Madonna went to Cannes in a cross-your-heart bra and girdle. The High Street took the hint, and with a bit of bravery, a bra can now be worn under an open shirt tied at the waist or beneath a shadowy organza body. Gossard's Wonderbra has had a remarkable revival in recent years, being worshipped for its secret padded ingredient, its bow nestling between the cups, the opaque lace and rounded shape. The secret is to counteract a bra's prettiness with tougher elements such as jeans, a leather or wool jacket and forget about the shirt in between. Less overtly sexy, but in the same mould, are pretty corsets, thermal camisoles and matching cardigans to wear with denims or slim cotton trousers. The crossover also works the other way round: the best slip dresses pay homage to the humble petticoat. The attraction: you're never quite sure!

Above *An eye for the boys that never loses sight of being a girl: wear a mannish suit, but soften the tie, keep shoes dainty and play up glamorous make-up. The interest is in the contrast.*

When underwear's so pretty, it's a shame to keep it just for intimate affairs.

Right *A satin slip turns inside out with lashings of pearls.*
Below *Only a shadowy body comes between a Wonderbra and daylight.*

THE BASIC WARDROBE: PLAN AND ACTION

Quality is always a better philosophy than quantity. It was once calculated that British women have something like three times more clothes than their French counterparts, but the French spend three times more! A French woman with flair may buy nothing other than a belt all season, but, though inevitably pricey, it will be a precision purchase. Always shop for your wardrobe rather than yourself. Don't buy something just because you like it but think how it will expand what you already have. Well-chosen separates ring more changes than co-ordinated outfits that look disjointed with anything else. Avoid extremes you'll tire of, but if something is a success, invest in two. Buy nothing until your basics are all there.

Bodies and leggings must contain the stretch ingredient Lycra to prevent bagging. Try to pick ones in slightly thicker, better fabrics, perhaps with a fine rib, which will conceal your underwear, sit well on your shoulders and bottom, and last. Both bodies and leggings form a compact, uncomplicated base on which you can put looser layers but still let people know you have a good figure. Everyone looks their best in them because they smooth out the lumps and bumps, though leggings in prints or in any colour other than black or navy rarely pay your bottom and thighs huge favours. The tightness of a body looks better with flared skirts than does a T-shirt because the waist is defined, and provides a sharp backdrop for a jacket opening with none of the clutter of a blouse. Bodies worn with leggings need a long, lean figure or a jacket that reaches well below your bottom. That way, they form a continuous block, like a catsuit, that's actually quite slimming, and with pretty shoes and jewellery quickly looks glamorous for evening.

T-shirts are most useful in white or a stripe. Other colours have a tendency to fade, and don't look as crisp. It's worth spending a pound or two extra on a good quality cotton and a neckline that holds its shape, but they should be cheap enough for you to have a cross-section of sleeve lengths, neck shapes—so you can play with necklaces and scarves—and sizes. A size too small and short will tuck into trousers and slip comfortably under jackets; a larger size worn loose is an easy way of wearing slim trousers, leggings or cycling shorts. Make sure you keep your T-shirts clean and supple; the minute they go grey, replace them.

Sweaters can behave like T-shirts, and there are more options in a broad range of different lengths and thicknesses. Try to have some long and loose to wear with leggings or show only a peep of skirt beneath, and others short and neat—maybe a skinnyrib— also to wear with leggings, if you have the figure, but mostly to tuck into trousers or go under a big tied shirt. Although oversized chunky cable knits are wonderfully cosy and look great with narrow pants, nothing is more quietly impressive than a simple fine wool knit in black, navy, a pastel or a shade on the cream-to-camel spectrum. Excessively ornate sweaters are limiting and all those Sloane Ranger animals and fruits knitted in rows, even Icelandic patterns, have been done to death. Know which neckline most suits you. A gaping sweater worn alone can look too bare with pale skin and needs the colour and textures of accessories or a jacket collar; a polo-neck may look sleeker with closely cropped hair or long hair that's tied back than with flowing tresses; a crewneck steers a sympathetic course for everyone.

Shirts should be crisp, and, of course, clean: because they are closest to your face, they are often the piece people notice most. They hand you a wealth of options, swinging wildly from the mannish to overtly feminine, from pure understated lines to

'The foundation pieces of a wardrobe are like old friends. You know the ones I'm talking about: the black body, the white body, leggings, the double-breasted jacket, the little black dress, the slip skirt, the front-drape skirt and trousers tailored like men's.'

DONNA KARAN,
DESIGNER

'I always buy the same things: navy blazers, navy and green sweaters, black turtlenecks, men's jackets, twin sets, white shirts, black pants and black ballerina pumps. Crazy things like plastic shirts, orange jackets and silver pants I end up giving away unworn.'

INÈS DE LA FRESSANGE,
DESIGNER AND FORMER
CHANEL HOUSE MODEL

foppish frills and flamboyant sleeves, from the oversized you wear loose or belt to the simple sleeveless one that slips inside a waistband. You should aim for a cross-section. The number of ways you can wear a white cotton man's shirt is untold, but stripes and pure bolts of colour also make for a quick way of changing your wardrobe dramatically. Against black or white, the effect of a shirt in a single bold colour is startling; pure pastel shades on the other hand—a lilac, an ice green, a powder blue—lend a tone of luxury; busy cartoon-print shirts look fabulous worn with single blocks of colour. Multiplied by variables like wearing masses of jewellery or none at all, wrapping the tails round the body so you criss-cross the bust, wearing the collar inside a jacket or out, over a sweater, body or T-shirt, or with a silk scarf or bandanna at the neck, the shirt is possibly the most versatile basic. Double-cuffs add an extra dimension and the choice between sleeves rolled up or ornamented with extravagant cuff links. A golden rule is to vary the fabrics. Wear a soft and fluid shirt one day, something sharp and starched as a contrast the next. Nothing beats cotton and linen when they're newly ironed; satin, organza and washed silks need careful handling, especially cautious washing and dry cleaning, but their opulence merits the effort.

Far left *The huggable sweater with leggings or slim trousers is great easy dressing, but mustn't look sloppy: highly polished lace-ups or dainty pumps, well-chosen accessories and good grooming make the difference.*

Left *The impact is in the simplicity.*

Above *A black body and leggings are a fail-safe base in which to root subsequent layers.*

Jackets should be your one extravagance. Whatever its shape—maybe a blazer, a cropped bellboy jacket, a safari, jean or sports jacket—a well-tailored jacket without braiding, pattern or fussy detail gives unity to separates dressing, and, worn with different proportions and the right accessories, can metamorphose admirably to suit changing fashions. It will double as a coat, yet is cool enough for summer and can provide the 'lift' you need, which includes a businesslike air when you want to make more of a statement. Its style, fabric and colour should be as simple and as versatile as possible without being boring. Because it's often the top layer on show, it's worth turning to designer ranges for the right cut and an interesting fabric. One jacket that fits perfectly is better than lots of cheaper ones that never quite make the grade, wear badly and soon look misshapen. Don't shy away from designer jackets because you think they'll be quirky and quickly date. Jacket shapes actually don't change much—it's the skirts that alter proportions and make news.

Skirts and trousers: lifestyle, job requirements and how comfortable they make you feel will determine the proportion of skirts to trousers in your wardrobe. You can't go wrong with a wool gabardine black skirt of a fashionable length and a pair of fairly narrow black crepe trousers, to be dressed up or down depending on the occasion. Thereafter, vary the shapes, fabrics and colours you buy—gradually move into brighter shades or a check, into flannel, linen, tweed, even washed silk, silk velvet and chiffon. 'Making a change in the skirt is one of the easiest and least costly ways to update a wardrobe,' said *Vogue* in 1991 when the skirt came out of its short and straight era and suddenly went light and swishy. The length and weight of your skirt and its relationship with the jacket, height of shoe, and density of stocking are the variables that pinpoint fashion. Some skirts are a problem to wear, such as the wrapover that just will not stay shut and the exceedingly short skirt that makes a few movements awkward. Opaque tights hold the key to modesty, but that doesn't solve the problem in summer. In general terms, a cheap skirt is less obvious than cheap trousers. To get the fit and fabric and half-lining that make trousers hang right, you have to spend more. Trousers are acceptable in almost every environment now—even in the office—and women love them because they give them the go ahead to move freely. So we don't tire of the same shapes, it's important to experiment beyond the broad and narrow into jodhpurs, Capri pants, pinstripes, and turn ups; mannish Oxford bags provide a striking counterpoint to a woman's body

Left *The fabric and length of skirt establish the mood.*

that is well worth exploiting. A sports jacket paired with trousers is a very different look from a trouser suit, which is simpler and sufficiently understated to make a fuss of a shirt or a floating chiffon or silk scarf, but that doesn't stop you wearing its components separately. As with skirts, the shoe issue is vital: only slim trousers can take a strappy high sandal or moderate mule; high sandals and court shoes with wide trousers tend to look stuffy, and flat pumps or boots with a heel are more suitable.

Coats that are simple and timeless enough to live in for six months of the year are classics. They have to suit every occasion - be neither too smart nor too untidy—and contain no dramatic fashion statements and fussy details like braiding or unusually shaped lapels, which are limiting. A man's overcoat is a lesson in how understated lines and base colour never look out of place. The female equivalent will be softer and less structured but follow similar, unpretentious principles. Judge the amount you spend on a coat by how much you will wear it, and go without until you find one you really love. For details on what to look for, see *The Classics*, pages 95-97.

MAKING A WARDROBE FASHIONABLE

The trump card is knowing where the emphasis lies: is the new look top heavy, or long and lean? Designers still might approve of leggings, for example, but what's new to make them less or more important? How is the essential body being worn—under a transparent or opaque shirt or on its own or always beneath a jacket? Are accessories the main issue? What size is the jewellery? Is it predominantly gilt, *faux* pearls, coloured stones or more based on natural themes? The height of shoes will alter proportions significantly. Boots, not shoes, may be crucial. Get it wrong, and you're soon out of date.

The pitfall lies in being badly informed. People are fond of saying that fashion goes round in circles. It doesn't. 'Long skirts are back,' they say glibly. 'Good job I kept mind from last time they were fashionable.' In fact, second time around they never look right. The new length may in fact be quite different. What looked perfect on the calf might now be an inch or two higher or touching the ankle bone. Minute adjustments alter proportions dramatically. The fabric, the cut and the way the skirt moves may have changed too: the longer lengths that hit the runways in 1991-2 were softer than their Seventies and Eighties counterparts, some in floaty materials, others more like a narrow riding

'Interior design magazines are very intuitive. You can find a purple sofa with mustard flowers, rich gemstone tones with pastels, and fabrics for interior decoration are superb points of reference— frequently adventurous and extremely lavish.'

JOSEPHINE TURNER,

FASHION RETAILER,

A LA MODE, LONDON

skirt, but all without exception had a high split that made them sexier than before. It's the subtleties that count.

Fashion colours are critical in pepping up a basic wardrobe. 'You may have a wardrobe full of black, navy, camel and white,' explains Josephine Turner, owner of top designer shop A La Mode, 'but when you add a colour that's important for the season, for example a pastel sweater, suddenly everything you have on is fashionable; no matter how old the other clothes you are wearing, people just look at that new colour.'

The eccentric fashion quirks that make the runway shows theatrical but find their way into the press are the ones you should always avoid. Firstly, they may be so radical they swamp your personality. Secondly, they probably won't survive much longer than a season. And thirdly, they can be formidably expensive. You and your friends will soon be sick of them and render them useless. Stick to progressive and subtle trends that are just as demonstrative without the hype.

COLOUR SENSE

For versatility and to avoid confusion, it's wise to have two or three base colours in your wardrobe and then ladle on perhaps only five or six variables. A random colour scheme is very limiting. Black, navy, camel, dark brown, or dark grey are the perfect backdrop for primaries, pastels and all the zillions of succulent shades in between. Black is a classic base for day and evening, and can make even the cheapest of clothes glamorous. All-black, however, can be deadening on anything but the most radiant complexion and needs lifting with another colour—say, via a brilliant shirt, handbag, a pair of gloves, a lipstick. White is one of the most striking contrasts and flatters everyone by reflecting light on to the face. Together, they work day or night.

Choosing shades that suit your skin tone or hair is a very outdated way of wearing colour. Some people do benefit from certain colours, but you can search for ever trying to find the right shade and it may not be fashionable anyway. It's less restricting to be unconventional. Pairing green with beige, or navy with cream are very average ways of putting colour together. Flick through art books for inspiration. Pop Artists' colour mixes are wholly different from those of the Impressionists; study how artists juxtapose colours to create moods. Nature, too, is a powerful teacher: it puts fresh leaves with berries and fruits; think of the reds and polished browns of autumn; the crisp contrasts of spring; the cool aquas, sand and deep azures of the coast.

'When I say "orange", I don't mean yellow-orange, I mean red-orange—the orange of Bakst and Diaghilev.'

DIANA VREELAND, FORMER EDITOR, AMERICAN *VOGUE*

Blending tones within the same colourway can be curiously soothing—from vanilla through oatmeal to camel, for example; from cobalt to sea green and turquoise. At the other pole, you can bounce colours that scream at the same pitch: hot orange with pink, citric lemon with lime, but never wear more than two at a time; any more and you'll look like a clown. The secret is to wear them with confidence. Most bright colours require a strong personality; adjust the quantity you use to suit your mood. Don't scrutinise a tweed suit for a fleck of perhaps purple and decide to 'match' it with a purple shirt, or co-ordinate an outfit too much—navy trimmed with red carried through into your hat, shoes and gloves. It's more inventive and less twee to oppose.

A good way of expanding your thoughts on colour is to be specific—not just red, but cranberry, claret or brick. It's an accurate means of carrying colour in your head, and teaches you to be selective, which stands the whole of your wardrobe in good stead.

Above *Texture blending is rich and sensuous. Here, Romeo Gigli puts brocade against fake fur against shot silk.*

PATTERNS AND TEXTURES

Designer Christian Lacroix especially has taught us to be open minded when it comes to mixing patterns and textures. His exotic print and playful juxtaposition of different fabrics and colour have spelt out in capital letters how fashion is at its best when it breaks all the rules. If worn confidently, unexpected mixes can be the most exciting, their novelty the spice in the pudding. Karl Lagerfeld at Chanel was one of the first to rejuvenate tweed suits by adding a stretch denim surprise element, and put patent on wool suits, biker leathers with tulle and taffeta ballroom skirts. Fashion journalists responded by coining a phrase—'tough against tender'—which told of designers' fresh approach. Gianni Versace has combined patterns as opposite as animal print and sea shells, whilst others clash the tartans, or work multi-sized checks, stripes and spots against each other, revelling in patterns that run at a tangent. That's not to give the go ahead for irrational, clownish behaviour—mixtures should say hello to each other but never fight; designers always have a well-monitored method in their seeming madness that makes the difference between being witty and just missing.

Above *Christian Lacroix's pattern-clash philosophy is rooted in wit not comedy.*

ACCESSORIES

The motto for accessories? Go for bold! Toppling texture and colour over a simple backdrop with beads and baubles or lashings of gilt is the point at which the fun really starts. A bite of colour

LUCINDA CHAMBERS CHOOSES

Lucinda Chambers is fashion director at British *Vogue*. 'I only buy things I consider intrinsically beautiful. That's why they're bound to go together. Some of my Georgina Von Etzdorf velvet scarves are so wonderful you could put them on a sofa, the window, not only on the body! I never buy anything that won't last or is bound to date, nothing garish that I'll tire of. I love mixing textures, dark jewel colours and the crispest whites and creams. Thirty per cent of my wardrobe is antique clothing, but I'd always wear an antique piece with the smartest thing I have.' When asked to pick ten versatile elements plus ten accessories from her wardrobe, she chose:

The versatile elements

- a white shirt

- white T-shirt

- High Street black leggings

- Chain-store navy soft wool jacket with tie belt

- Antonio Fusco lilac double-breasted jacket, feminine and smart

- Ralph Lauren hessian, long, slim skirt

- silk velvet patterned tunic in dark greens and burgundy

- antique beaded vest, chestnut colour

- Oxford bags

- men's chunky soft wool cream trousers with turn-ups

The accessories

- matt gold drop earrings of different-sized spheres

- diamanté daisy earrings

- aluminium beads threaded on a leather thong

- turquoise beads from India

- ethnic stone and silver ring

- organza stoles—one pearl grey, one blue/green, one creamy patterned

- Fair Isle beret

- a pack of tweed-look speckly socks in red/green, purples and mixed browns

- black velvet flat pumps

- rich brown, lace-up ankle boots with pointed toes

Putting them into the blender

- For work: beaded vest, navy jacket, Oxford bags, ring, boots, aluminium beads

- The weekend/country: T-shirt, wool trousers, navy jacket, red/green speckled socks, velvet pumps, beret, aluminium beads

- For shopping: white shirt, hessian skirt, navy jacket, turquoise beads, diamanté daisy earrings, boots

- The interview: long lilac jacket, neat leggings, an organza scarf, gold earrings, boots

- A party: velvet tunic, leggings, organza scarf, ring, gold earrings, boots

on a tiny bag or earrings can energise black, break up the monotony of a calculated look, or join in a party of multi-patterns. Accessories are about the imagination, a nod back to the dressing-up box when you pile on personality. Why be discreet?

The number of permutations possible by simply combining your accessories and clothes are enormous. Think how many looks you could conjure from your jewellery, scarves, gloves shoes, belt, hat and tights with a white shirt for example; every piece has a character you can add or subtract to determine the final impression. Use accessories to draw attention from a part of you you're less than happy about, but don't complicate the impact of beautiful clothes with pieces that are over fussy. The right jewellery can make a simple cheap dress; the wrong jewellery can destroy even the most expensive one. Try to focus on just one or two areas—any more and you can kill them all; for example, if you wear a hat and a choker, don't bother with the big dangly earrings. What's great about accessories is that they seldom wear out and rarely date, so are sound investments.

Below *Accessories pick you out from the crowd.*

Costume jewellery's rule is the bigger the better. Winding strands and strands of, say, pearls or glass beads round the neck like a choker makes a greater statement and is more luxurious than a single demure row.

Worn singularly, the intrinsic beauty of one piece is key: an exquisite cuff; a large drop sculpted from silver or gold, or a piece of amber can be impressively simple on a long leather thong or black cord. Natural elements like a small piece of driftwood or glass can be reinvented as beautiful adornments. The mood is quietly emphatic. Ethnic jewellery is wonderful, but there is so much around now that you have to wear big, unusual pieces to be individual; if you buy them abroad, make a level-headed decision that they won't look wrong when you get back home. High Street multiples and department stores are lucky dips for jewellery, but try not to buy metals that are too shiny and look cheap; matt may have a more quality appearance. Scavenging antique markets for forgotten pieces, resetting old rings, breaking up necklaces to pick out perfect beads, tying knots between them to alter the way they hang, are all inventive tricks of the trade.

Shoes on the High Street come in great shapes, but they nearly always look best in dark colours, especially black; the subtle shades of expensive ranges rarely translate well into middle-market lines—if you see them, grab them! Very cheap shoes are false economy; leather will look good long after synthetic shoes have fallen apart, so it's worth saving up for two or three good pairs; In fact, dark brown leather improves with age when polished like a shiny conker. Fragile extravaganzas in satin and silk look wonderful in the box and when first worn, but are impossible to keep pristine, and pale shoes, however small, inevitably look big. Venture into different shapes that show style—a medium-height fine slingback, a mule, a moccasin, a unique heel. The height and weight of the shoe alter the proportions of your clothes substantially and in some seasons may be the only dramatic changes a designer makes. A short skirt with high shoes may need a longer jacket; with a long skirt, ankle boots, whatever the height, have a different effect from strappy sandals. The mood switches, but doesn't fall neatly into high heels for business or evening, low for casual: a medium heel dresses up leggings, but where you wear them is up to you.

Hosiery needs careful consideration and should never be an afterthought: black opaque tights worn with black shoes and a black skirt elongates your appearance and draws attention to the

'Small jewellery is pretentious, has no humour and is swamped by your personality. A bit of bad taste is no bad thing, but you have to wear it with confidence!'
VICTOIRE DE
CASTELLANE,
HEAD OF JEWELLERY
DESIGN, CHANEL

Above *Against a pure silhouette, shells on a cord are fragile and strong.*

jacket or shirt you wear on top—you're using the continuous colour almost as a plinth; put sheer tights with the same clothes, and the look is divided, and each section comes under scrutiny. Dark opaque tights are flattering for chubby legs and, though the initial outlay seems steep, are economical since they rarely ladder. Good quality pairs don't let any skin tone show through, even when stretched, and Lycra is the ingredient that solves the problem of bags and creases round the knees and ankles. Sheer tights are elegant but less forgiving, though a high heel will stretch the calf muscle and make your legs look slimmer. To look even, sheer tights should be really fine—ten, seven, even five denier, and some companies have answered the question of durability with a high denier knit that has the appearance of a more fragile denier. The danger zones? Textured and shiny tights are too distracting—the latter appear striped in photographs—and no tight is sufficiently natural to survive the open-toed sandal!

Hats can add wit to your wardrobe. Provided you don't feel self-conscious and look awkward, an informal hat with character has tremendous style. A beret imbues all the sex appeal of Faye Dunaway in *Bonnie and Clyde*, a trilby provides that dose of masculinity that's so attractive on women, the creaminess of a soft panama is a sudden burst of summer that flatters every skin tone. A plain wide-brimmed straw has wonderful crisp lines that emphasise the eyes and lips; it can be dressed up with elaborate hat pins, feathers and clouds of tulle, but the key word has to be big. Don't be afraid of height especially if you're fairly short: a low crown with a high-collared coat can make you appear squat.

Scarves are one of the best vehicles for attaching bolts of colour or different textures to your clothes. A scarf can pull many faces: one minute it's a headband, the next a hair tie, a French kerchief, a stole, even a belt to wear with jeans; wear one inside a partly open shirt, line the lapels of a jacket outside or just in, give a long coat a panel of drama, rather like the trim on a bishop's cope. To work them to the maximum, scarves should be of different lengths and fabrics. Play them against each other in layers to peel off glamorously; worn singularly, make sure they have impact—for example, realise the surprise value of organza and chiffon's night-time spirit when worn with a structured wool trouser suit.

Belts draw attention to the waist, that's a fact. But it's less clear whether that is always a good thing. Some waistlines do not stand up to being made a fuss of and do well to hand over the point of

'I love the contrast between dressy clothes and no jewellery, and austere clothes with glamorous jewellery.'

NATHALIE HAMBRO,
FREELANCE STYLIST

emphasis to parts of the body in better condition. Sometimes the waist is not the central point of fashion: generally, short skirts are trying to emphasise the hips and legs, long skirts play up the waist. Belts can interrupt a look whose strength is its unbroken smooth vertical line. They're not simply a way of keeping your trousers up—if trousers don't stand up of their own accord, you haven't chosen a good fit; rather, belts should be the result of a conscious decision to add a colour and texture, perhaps a jewelled or exquisitely carved buckle that makes a spectacular centrepiece, to finish off the tops of skirts and trousers and create a narrow point against which flared skirts and shirts look more dramatic. Always check before you buy a pair of trousers, that the belt loops will fit your belts; without the loops, belts seldom sit still and wander up to annoy you. Most belts come in different sizes and you should always buy one that's exactly right—if you have to add more holes the chances are, when you've buckled it, you'll have more left over than you know what to do with. Black and nutty brown leather belts are the most useful: cowboy style with a silver tooled buckle for jeans; slimmer, smoother and more elegant ones for classic clothes. Suede belts tend to rub and shine on the edges; broad patent is a glossy contrast over black crepe or a colour; metal chain belts—in silver, gilt, sometimes with pearls and colourful baubles—sitting on the hips and draped over the stomach pinch a glamorous look from Chanel.

Bags are a problem: you want them to cope with everyday needs, but you don't want to be bogged down with excess baggage. Bags were once way at the bottom of the shopping agenda: yes, we would invest in new clothes, shoes, even different hats, but our one and only bag had to survive every occasion until it died. Now there's a wide choice and we can change them daily to suit our clothes and mood. The frivolous bag of toy-town proportions, maybe in satin and hung with beads, is witty and forces us to edit out all the superfluous paraphernalia we're tempted to carry round with us, but it's too fragile and cute for work. Big totes and back packs can cope with all our lifestyles, with enough room for Filofax, exercise clothes and make-up bag, but a handheld bag of moderate proportions with a tiny handle goes easier on the shoulder and, swung at the end of an extended arm or looped over one at right angles, looks equally stylish and modern. Like shoes, handbags look better quality and are most versatile in black, and benefit from the extra you pay for good leather. They may seem expensive but, unlike shoes, bag shapes don't change that much and with care could last a lifetime.

'Look out for the key elements of the season you can add to your basics. It may be the right-shaped trousers or a new length of skirt—either way it says that you're in the know.'

VANESSA DE LISLE,

FASHION CONSULTANT,

HARRODS

UNDER STATEMENTS

What goes on under your clothes is just as critical as what goes on top. Underwear that fits badly creates unnecessary bulges and shows through your clothes. A bra should always be tried on and fitted properly by a trained assistant; it's no good assuming you're a particular size because the bras in department stores are made by individual manufacturers and sizing is variable, so be prepared to be measured each time. Too large a bra and you're left with extra cloth that puckers through your clothes; too small and the result is two bosoms over the top, maybe two at the side, as well as the two Nature gave you! Don't be afraid of a strong bra. Seamless bras are terrible to fit; the bosom drops, which leaves a gap at the top, and there is nothing to hide the nipples. Underwired bras are best for most people, but check the wires don't land on you when you move; lift your arms, touch your toes, really put a bra through its paces before you part with a penny. All bras can go a bit loose in the wash, so make sure you keep adjusting the straps—but don't shorten them so much you fall out underneath. Try to have a wide selection to suit your clothes: low-back ones, slightly larger ones for pre-menstrual days when your shape may alter, sports bras, and padded ones that are pretty enough to wear on their own or under an open shirt.

Tiny bikini briefs might be good for the ego but a larger size or waist-level pants with high-cut legs may do more to avoid the ugly underwear ridge that shows through trousers and skirts. 'There are second-skin full- or half-slips with inbuilt pants and bras on the market now, which are smoother under skirts,' says June Kenton of top corsetiers Rigby & Peller, 'and bodies with cycling-short bottoms for under trousers. If you have tummy rolls and a sizeable bottom, bodies will make you look leaner than pants and a bra, which only push the rolls together.' G-strings are used by models under close observation on the runways and are invisible under leggings. Alternatively, wear tights that have a cotton gusset.

Left Bags used to be essentially practical – now they're a source of decoration too.

Above Unforgettable underwear is the sort you can forget about.

TRAVELLING RIGHT

The art of packing for a holiday follows the same principles that apply to the rest of your wardrobe. In fact, selecting clothes that are few enough to fit a suitcase but fulfil every eventuality is the perfect training ground for your wardrobe at home. The first rule is to do your homework. Work out what life's going to be like at the other end of the flight: there's no sense in arriving with

TAKING CARE OF CLOTHES: THE CHECKLIST

• Hang up clothes as soon as you take them off: when they're warm the creases drop out more easily; empty the pockets so they don't get misshapen; brush well before putting in the wardrobe.

• Tissue around wire hangers will soften the ridges they make on clothes.

• Don't wear the same clothes or shoes two days running.

• Place a bowl of water next to clothes that have been in a smoky atmosphere.

• Always let deodorants and scents dry before you dress, or they could leave a stain. Perspiration smells on washable clothes, however, can be treated with a roll-on deodorant, washed, then rinsed in vinegar and water.

• To keep the moths away, don't keep dirty clothes in the wardrobe or let them linger at the bottom of a laundry basket; pine cones are sweeter-smelling deterrents than mothballs.

• Shoes: a pencil rubber will remove any scuffs on suede; put polish on leather the night before so it really soaks in, then shine; Nivea cream will substitute for polish in an emergency; use shoe trees or crumpled tissue to stuff the toes and sprinkle in potpourri to keep them smelling sweet; wooden, not plastic, shoe trees will absorb any sweat; never dry wet shoes by a radiator or fire, which will overdry the leather and make it crack.

• Skirts: 'Pack full evening skirts with bunched up tissue and then put them in a bag to prevent them getting dusty,' advises Fay Appleby, ex-dresser to the Princess of Wales. 'Pleated skirts should be concertinaed inside a stocking to keep the pleats sharp.'

• Coats should be cleaned and bagged at the end of winter, or covered with a pinned sheet.

• Sweaters will 'bobble' less if they have a short spell in the freezer, or if turned inside out before washing and lightly ironed on the wrong side; woollens that have shrunk can be restored to their original size by finishing off a wash with clean soap suds instead of clear water.

• Washing: 'Check the instructions!' pleads Mario Michael of Haywards Specialist Dry Cleaners in Knightsbridge. 'Wet one corner and iron between pieces of white cloth to test the colour fastness of a fabric, and when the dye is likely to run, hand wash in potato water.' Underwired bras are best machine washed in a bag; if you hand-wash them, you'll wring out, and bend the wires.

• Dry cleaning: attach labels on stains saying exactly what they are.

• Ironing: check labels for temperatures; don't wear something immediately after ironing or it'll crush more; put a towel in the sleeve of a jacket so you don't iron in a knife crease; scorch marks should be dampened in glycerine and water, then soaked in borax; to restore the finish on shiny trouser seats when pressing, apply white vinegar with a sponge; vinegar's also good for helping a hemline disappear, hanging clothes in a steamy bathroom will make creases drop out.

armloads of cases expecting to be picked up by car if the only mode of transport is a minibus from a bus stop miles away. Find out, too, if there's a dress code you should follow: some countries won't appreciate skimpy shorts and bare arms. Then choose pieces that are neither crushable nor bulky. Limit sweaters to one and a soft cardigan for chilly evenings, and then go for leggings, bodies, stretch trousers, man-made fibres and the softest panama—anything that smooths out when you wear it. The quiet purity of cream, white, pastels and sea-breeze blues is perfect for holidays, pepped up with ginghams, stripes and spots; navy mixed in looks crisp, but black can be hot and dusty. Next, think about elements you can dress up or down with costume jewellery and long, fine stoles: the T-shirts, the white shirts, an unstructured jacket, loose thin cricket trousers, a sleeveless dress. Long, wraparound skirts, or lengths of fine fabric knotted at your waist are deliciously relaxing in hot climates, are curiously cooler than brief scraps and also almost always more elegant. The shoes you choose should be varied and light: thong sandals suit both sightseeing and evening; newly whitened plimsolls look crisp and are more comfortable when worn with the laces removed; a pretty strappy sandal or a medium-heeled bright mule are luxuries, but great for dressing up neat capri pants or an ankle-length split skirt for dinner, even lunch by the pool!

Below *Perfect packing is a case of careful editing.*

PACKING MAKES PERFECT

A tall, narrow case is easier to carry than a broad holdall that bangs against your legs. Pack your shoes first, in shoe bags preferably, and stuff them with tights and socks to save space and keep their shape. Knitwear and non-crushable fabrics go in next, laid flat, folded bottom to top, with sleeves in a V. Then trousers and skirts, folded at hip level not down the leg, perhaps with sweaters in the fold to soften the crease. Next pack the jacket, buttoned and folded once widthways, face up. Shirts and T-shirts that crush most easily form the top layer. Underwear will pad out the gaps, and is easier to find if kept in bags. Belts should run round the inside walls of the case. If space is really tight, clothes rolled and arranged in rows take up less room and emerge virtually uncreased.

Always fold *into* a suitcase, rather than transferring clothes ready folded, when they rarely fit. Tissue paper between layers will help prevent creasing. Hair dryers, make-up and other hard things like cameras, even shoes, are really best in a separate small bag to take on the plane as hand luggage. A hair dryer is doubly valuable in that it will blow-dry out creases, but, before you leave, check its voltage is compatible with that used at your destination. The final step: slip in a foldable bag for extra pieces you acquire while away.

SHOPPING LOGIC

In theory, shopping is one of life's pleasures. In reality, it's perplexing. Emotionally, a mixed bag. Economically, a minefield. Psychologically, a pendulum that swings with your mood. We've all been there. The compliments, the confusion, the all-time lows. Part of the problem is that we tend to play mind games with clothes, treading a fine line between those that are a figment of our imagination and those that actually exist. By not taking it seriously enough we make far too many compromises on quality, allow ourselves to be swayed by persuasive sales talk or worse, are nudged into worthless purchases by our own miscalculation. We do no groundwork yet expect to perform miracles in a lunch hour. Let's get one thing straight: strategic thinking is rooted in the well-dressed woman's psyche. Good buying, like good grooming, is an acquired skill.

Left *Shopping can seriously affect your bank balance and well being, but remember to keep your sense of humour.*

STRATEGIC THINKING

Behind every stylish woman lies a steely determination to get what she wants. For the evidence, watch the international experts at work. A national pastime? More a profession. The Italian cruises the piazzas day in, day out until she finds the perfect buy. The Parisian, by her own admission, is ruthlessly discriminating, impossible and demanding by turns. The Manhattanite, whose expectations are based on performance and practicality, chooses clothes that are comfortable, uncreasable, designed to make an impact in the boardroom and are capable of switching roles at the weekend. For the New Yorker, the same garment must come complete with a guarantee that it can be added to three seasons later, or it won't even be considered.

Mistakes are made on a whim. They creep up on us, disarming, disconcerting and difficult to forget. A shopping strategy eliminates errors and evolves out of plain common sense. Think realistically. A considered plan to find a plain pair of linen trousers is far more likely to come to fruition than setting your sights on an imaginary jacket. Remember the trickle-down effect of fashion. What starts out totally out of reach tends to find its way—in diluted form—on to the High Street.

The first step is to eradicate the automatic link between shopping and spending—one need not necessarily involve the other. Draw on your past experiences and learn from, rather than repeat them. Second, research. So long as it is taken at a leisurely pace, even the most meticulous groundwork won't feel like hard slog and it can save an enormous amount of footwork. Start by scanning magazines, and buying the right newspapers at the right time (approximately eight weeks out of fifty-two contain collection reports). Reject the headline-makers, the loss-leaders and unwearables. Decipher the major themes, then decide on what you can actually envisage fitting into your lifestyle by flashing back to your wardrobe. Sandwiched between the visuals are the hard facts on new shop openings, and changes of addresses of stockists. Photographs are incredibly deceptive. Therefore if you are buying on the basis of a picture, always take note of the caption, which will tell you the type of fabric, give an accurate description of colour, and describe the parts you cannot see.

Identifying your buying potential is the most crucial factor in balancing spending and is normally a case of knowing what you can and cannot afford. One of the biggest pitfalls is false economy. Apply exactly the same standards of discipline and discrimination to designer and chain-store garments. Illogical

Right Think carefully before you spend. The most valuable investment you can make is taking time out to plan a strategy.

thinking has serious consequences—purchasing yet another white shirt, misjudging your taste level. Unwise buys, large and small, add up to the same conclusion: a receding bank balance and a wardrobe of unwearable clothes.

The actual shopping process takes a separate set of skills. First rule: dress appropriately. This will put you in the right frame of mind. Difficult, if you have to squeeze your shopping into a working day. Basically, what you wear should always relate to the kind of styles you are looking for. As a general rule, dress simply. There is nothing more exasperating than struggling with a multi-layered outfit, particularly at high noon in a communal changing room. If you are on the lookout for a garment to pair with one you already own, wear it, or at least take it along. Even a photographic memory won't bring the finer details—exact shade, proportion—to mind. Always keep jewellery to a minimum—apart from the obvious security risk, it tends to click fabric, and wastes time putting on and taking off.

Think carefully about which accessories you wear. Comfortable shoes are essential, but bear in mind that heel height alters proportions dramatically—a flat brogue with a little black dress gives the totally wrong impression of how it will balance with a strappy evening shoe. Make sure your hosiery is compatible when trying shoes. Take along a pair of socks or wear thicker tights if you are buying boots. Your feet expand as the day goes on and therefore trying later will give a more realistic indication of fit. Shoulder bags give the most accessibility because they leave your hands free. Use one with adequate compartments to separate your make-up from cheque cards and take only the things you are likely to use that day. Do you usually shop solo? A second opinion is often helpful, particularly if you are investing. Take a notebook along and use it to jot down ideas, plan where to go, calculate the cost—far safer and cheaper than a chequebook.

Left *Few can afford the luxury that good service brings. The higher the price tag, the greater the level of service.*

BUYING POWER

Money management is akin to time management. In one corner is Superwoman who is clever enough to juggle a gym class, a career and two children into a twenty-four-hour period; in the other, Ms Disorganised, who can't fit a facial into a blank weekend. Likewise, money—the amount is irrelevant: it's planning and organisation that count. Marital status dictates priorities— single women, particularly those in high-powered positions, will inevitably allocate a larger amount to their wardrobe—but age and lifestyle determine individual buying patterns.

As a starting point, assess specific regular monthly outgoings—mortgage, rent, insurance, bills, travel, expenses on top. That total minus your salary, grant or allowance could leave a tiny sum for clothes. But look beyond the calculations. Monitor your spending for a few months, draw up a cash timetable and watch the results. Do you nosedive into your savings on days when your confidence plummets or the split second your salary boosts your bank account? Do you splash out only at sale time? Is your spending as erratic as your taste level?

Buying patterns must be recognised before they can be restructured. Carefully assess the amount you are able to afford - however large or small. This could be on a weekly, monthly, or even yearly basis. Allow for impulse buys. The reasoning is not to instil a regimental mentality to buying, only a reasonable amount of restraint. Overspending has specific causes, and being constantly overdrawn could be put down to purchasing at the wrong time. It may be worth your while to open a separate account into which a set amount of money is transferred each month, or an account with certain shops where you are a regular customer. Credit cards can be lethal. By lulling you into a false sense of security (you are, after all, parting with plastic, not hard cash), it is all too easy to let the concept of what you can afford get out of hand. The only method of removing interest rates is to be totally disciplined and use strictly on a month-to-month basis. Accumulate a high bill and all you are effectively doing is paying off interest. Shop accounts severely restrict where you buy and persuade you to make purchases because they give you more time to pay. Choose wisely—don't be tempted to open an account on the strength of a few successful buys. Accounts are long-term options, and should only be considered after a rapport has been established. Note the interest rates—the convenience of a card could mean you end up paying way over the odds for your clothes.

Mood swings and specific seasons trigger excess spending. The shopaholic is particularly vulnerable during the pre-holiday period. Absolutely convinced she can't possibly set foot on a plane without new holiday wardrobe, the list inevitably includes most of the things already in her possession: a swimsuit/pair of cotton drill shorts/a dozen new T-shirts. The result: a last-minute spending spree that costs more than the air fare. The chances are if you are the kind of woman who can recite the exact balance in your account at a split second's notice, you will also know how much you can realistically afford to spend on clothes. But disciplined spending is one thing, determining whether a purchase is a sound investment is another.

SERVICE

Good or bad service has a direct effect on our well-being. Like fast food, fast fashion has no time for niceties. What you pay for is exactly what you get. At a high-turnover shop where clothes are cheap, there is probably a tiny budget set aside for staff training. At worst, expect to be pursued by a trainee assistant (inevitably spurred on by the prospect of commission), who insists on offering you the benefit of his or her fashion analysis. At best, assistants are trained to tune into the individual customer, and react accordingly, understanding that for every woman who wants help at hand, there will be those that don't. The flip side of the argument is that sales staff have a raw deal, being at the receiving end of customer queries and endless complaints on why there are no size 12s left in stock. However, the sad fact remains that with few exceptions, good service is going out of style.

Yet, the ball is in your court. Take matters into your own hands: although no amount of reason will deter unwanted attention, if you need help, ask. Don't waste time sifting through racks of clothes in the vague hope of coming across the correct size. Unless you have telepathic qualities, there is no way you will find the right item without insider knowledge.

Consider the changing rooms. The communal kind built into almost every High Street shop is guaranteed to strike fear in the heart of most women—even those in the teen- or twenty-age bracket, with physiques in peak condition. More often than not, they are poorly designed, without space to step back, move freely and get a distanced view. Occasionally chain-store architects have made provisions for individual changing rooms—with wide, full-length mirrors if you are fortunate; in those without, the customer faces the nighmare scenario of having to parade in full view of what seems like every shopper in town. There is no real solution to this dilemma, except making life easier by avoiding peak times and requesting privacy whenever possible.

You are at your most susceptible when treading the fine line between buying something or not. Never allow yourself to be bulldozed into saying yes when your gut reaction says no. Whatever the circumstances, ignore the temptation to buy without trying on—legally, retailers are not obliged to refund money unless the garment is damaged. Exchanges and refunds in other cases are purely at the discretion of the shop. Eliminate spur-of-the-moment decision-making by allowing sufficient breathing space—ask the assistant to put clothes aside for a day or so to give yourself valuable thinking time. Even impulse buys can wait.

Right *It's up to you: shop alone, or take a friend along.*

Great service extends far beyond the boundaries of good manners. Top of the list: alterations. Tuned-in department stores employ in-house seamstresses who will note alterations on the spot; chain stores vary. Some shops run their own information service — dates of forthcoming sales, what stock is coming in, and the top of the range retailers will bend backwards to help, including delivering direct to your door.

SALE MANŒUVRES

The trouble with sales is that they are totally irresistible. Fever pitch atmosphere and lack of reasoning collide just as you confront the classic sale-time dilemma: a designer garment, slashed to a fraction of the full price. The compromises start: it is the wrong colour (you will grow to love it), the sleeves are too short (they can be let down) and you can't quite envisage where it will be worn (but you are convinced the right occasion will occur sometime in the future). Stop. The scene is set for yet another bargain buy that ends up at the back of the wardrobe. The reason being that it simply isn't the way you would act under normal circumstances. Why make those decisions because the price tag is reduced? Keep a cool head. The lure of purchasing pieces that are normally totally out of your price point is tempting enough. But any sale item—even one for a fraction of the original full price—is money badly spent if it proves to be unsuitable.

Flash back to the pre-sale period. The discerning shopper monitors the stock, picks out one or two pieces that are possibles and understands that although the key classics have probably been snapped up at full price, one or two may survive to sale time. She knows that cut-price merchandise can include loss leaders that were bought in to perk up the department (ideal for mannequins but unwearable on humans) or items that even the well-heeled customers shunned as vastly overpriced. Damaged or soiled garments that are in need of serious overhaul can be non-starters. Be discriminating about dirt. A grubby jacket that was once gleaming white, for example, is highly unlikely, even after meticulous cleaning, ever to regain its original sparkle. There are a few exceptions: cleanable dark shades or coloured fabrics (cotton for example) that can be washed in hot water and starched back to life. Knitwear is particularly tricky. Typically enticing: a bargain-priced cashmere sweater, near-perfect bar a tiny hole in a place that isn't on full view (say, at the back of the neck). Under those circumstances, buy it, but only on the condition that it will be invisibly and securely mended immediately. Wear the sweater without stitching it up first, and even the most minuscule pinprick turns into an irreparable ladder. Only consider damaged sale goods if they can realistically be put right. Be honest: if it can't be saved, reject it. Outerwear, especially jackets, where the damage is limited to the inside, falls into the category of maybe's. You will often find a coat that is immaculate from the outside, but greatly reduced because the lining is ripped or frayed. Never, unless you are an expert seamstress, buy a jacket or coat where the lapel is coming apart (only those with insider knowledge of collar construction will be able to repair it). Jersey is sewn with specialist machinery, therefore a circular skirt that needs a few centimetres off the length will probably prove more bother than it is worth. By the law of averages, there are sure to be great elements that have survived the season. It is up to you to separate the good from the bad.

BEST BARGAIN ADVICE

'If you have a limited amount of money to spend, always buy something permanent, seasonless—a beautifully cut, good basic, a wonderful plain jacket, coat, blazer or skirt. Spend wisely—don't pass up the opportunity of buying a jacket for half the normal price, but only if you are sure you will wear it. Amusing clothes are only worth buying if you have a wardrobe large enough for them to fit in.'

Josephine Turner,

Fashion Retailer,

A La Mode,

London

'I try to restrain myself from buying things that are really good value, but have enough of already—splashing out on yet another pair of grey flannel trousers is pointless. Work out what is coming into fashion and what's not—what you really need. The great buys are coats, cashmere, little black dresses, a tuxedo suit, anything by Jean Muir, a navy suit from YSL. Sales are golden opportunities to buy something fun—a beaded cardigan or classic jacket in a bright colour you can wear with lots of other things.'

Vanessa de Lisle,

Fashion Consultant,

Harrods

'Put the sale environment to the back of your mind. Ask yourself if you would actually pay full price for it. The worst mistakes are made with colour—a lime green jacket just because it has a 50 per cent reduction. Don't choose designers you have never had any experience with. The classic mistake is intending to slim into a smaller size. Make sure the garments fits, and always steer clear of clothes that are identifiable only with that season's look.'

Rita Britton,

Fashion Retailer,

Pollyanna,

Barnsley

MAINSTREAM SHOPPING

Designer shops . . .

. . . are magnetic, intimidating, and all too often, out of bounds, but not all designer stores are scary. Dispel your preconceptions of alluring exterior, imposing interior and price points spiralling towards the outer stratosphere, and you may be surprised to feel at one with the surroundings. They are skilfully designed to create a certain style, and to achieve the right atmosphere: the Japanese shop, airily understated with minimal pieces per square metre of floor space; Armani, cool and uncluttered to merge with the merchandise; Ralph Lauren's comfy country-house look with antique memorabilia and sink-in sofas; Chanel, a mirror image of the Parisian salon. It's easy to be anonymous in most places, but set one foot in the designer door and you're instantly conspicuous. The reasons for this are plain: the merchandise is almost impossible to live up to, and as a designer voyeur, the sales staff can sense you won't be buying. Don't be intimidated; it

Right *Designer clothes can afford to be simple because the fabric and finish are superlative.*

costs nothing to look. Living a vacuum existence, only scouring places within a certain price ratio is counter-productive. Seeing perfection has positive repercussions, partly in justifying the price, but by raising expectations it gives you the ammunition to become more discriminating when it comes to selecting cheaper clothes. Take the Alaïa dress where each seam is flatlocked to perfection—you now know there is no excuse for puckered seamlines, even in the most inexpensive pair of leggings.

Multiple designer shops—where a selection of status labels live happily together—are a great initiation ground and usually far less imposing than single name boutiques. The only drawback is that space allocation for each individual designer is fairly limited and as each garment is chosen purely at the discretion of the buyers, you must be in tune with their taste level. In these kind of stores, the secret weapon is superb service. The rapport between customer and sales staff is essential because it works both ways - feedback tells the buyers what is likely to sell, and in turn the customer is sure to find a look she is happy with. Here, you are likely to have the undivided attention of the assistant and more importantly, to be offered an unbiased opinion. This is not multiple-sales territory, where high turnover is the main priority. In designer shops, the individual matters. A disastrous sale or a disgruntled customer is seriously damaging.

Chain stores . . .
. . . are everywoman—affordable clothes for all walks of life, at any level of the social strata. Regardless of whom it is aiming at, each chain store has the same starting point: design teams who travel the world to gather ideas, investigate fabric fairs, and most importantly, scrutinise the international catwalks—what the top designers are up to is always the prime source of inspiration. How that directive is interpreted gives chain stores individual identity. Each chain handles the information differently: the chains appealing to the younger market may offer a Gaultier-like jacket at an affordable price; those catering for an older clientele, an inexpensive version of an Armani.

Chain-store shopping requires skill and intuition. The main drawback is in the choosing. Because it is an impossibility to keep pace with all of them, and easy to become complacent about which ones to visit, dismissing certain shops as out of your age or price range is convenient but not necessarily sound shopping sense. Design teams and direction change, and the original customer targetted may not be the one they are aiming at now.

It is not only price points that distinguish the shops but the design, quality and sizing of their stock. A company attracting the teenage market will cut its patterns smaller than one directed at the over-thirties. Switched-on chains understand that even generous cutting can't possibly accommodate every conceivable shape and size, and go one stage further offering a choice of leg length and an extended size range. An instantly identifiable signature is a plus, but also a problem in that you are likely to come face to face with a copy. At all costs avoid simulated haute couture where the mass market tries to take a shortcut with specialist techniques—bias cutting looks unbelievably tacky if not done properly. Buy instead basic pieces, particularly in stretch jersey—T-shirts, bodies, leggings—that could pass for designer.

Understatement is alien to the chain-store. You won't get clothes with the kind of subtleties and detail found in designer garments, which are not instantly recognisable yet send price points soaring. In contrast, the chain store design psyche centres on instant attraction. The universal attitude: if it costs, it must be seen. Hanger appeal is important, and interesting detail is often limited to the front: a jacket with lots of trimming at the collar, or a sweater with unusual stitchwork that extends no further than the shoulderline.

But, as chains compete for customers, there has been a gradual rise in quality. One of the most marked changes is that reputable traditional cloths are being used in the production of mass-market clothing. Discerning women are aware that the key fabrics making their debut in recent years have been Harris Tweed, pure wool and luxurious hand-washable silk.

Many designers have branched out into new areas, creating the atmosphere of a shopping mall within the confines of a High Street store. The discovery of the concept of 'total lifestyle' has revolutionised chain stores. It works on the assumption that if you feel an affinity with a particular designer's clothes, you will have a similar attraction to anything else he or she will produce. A prime example is Laura Ashley where the corporate signature filters into fabrics, fragrance and furniture.

Department stores . . .

. . . cut corners by doing the selecting for you. In terms of convenience, they eliminate unnecessary footwork. As opposed to spending a busy day trekking from one end of town to another, you find all the season's best buys under one roof. Department stores may save on travelling time, but unless you are familiar with the layout, knowing where to look can be confusing. Avoid

Above *Good tailoring is difficult to find because our bodies are rarely uniform in size.*

the great mistake of immediately making a bee-line for one particular department—tunnel vision can mean you bypass hidden surprises. To make shopping easier, garment types are grouped together—lingerie, hosiery, swimwear, millinery, with a selection of top brands on display. Different price ranges are located on alternate levels and particular groups of labels (e.g. the classics or young designer names) in small collections so that the customer has a wider variety of choice.

Great department stores offer everything from designer labels to diffusion lines, through to their own lower-priced brands. Although all buyers see the same collections, what they select differs radically. Department stores are by far the best place to find diffusion lines. By definition, these are the affordable versions of designer labels. Donna Karan's DKNY range and Arabella Pollen's Pollen B are examples of a growing trend in accessible designer wear. The main distinction between the designer and diffusion ranges is that although the basic direction is the same, the way the garment is executed is different. Cheaper cloth, less expensive detail and shapes with a younger, sportier feel are hallmarks of diffusion ranges.

Mail order
Buying clothes by post has one great plus. It is the only method by which a wardrobe can be chosen from the comfort of your home. The time factor has its ups and downs: the advantage is it gives you unlimited hours to browse and plan (which should wipe away the impulse buy); the disadvantage is the delay (anything from a few days to a few weeks) in receiving the goods.

Mail-order buying works on the same principle as selecting from a magazine—the decision to buy or not to buy is based purely on a photograph. Theoretically, postal fashion should cost less. Selling direct cuts out the middle-man and the overheads incurred by retail premises, but this isn't always the case. To combat the discrepancies in colour reproduction (one of the main reasons for customer dissatisfaction), many catalogues now have fabric swatches attached to give a clearer indication of the shade and type of cloth—closeups and diagrammatic layouts showing detail and the range of colours helps. Sizing charts are often included, but because fit varies considerably, finding the right one is often a case of trial and error.

Mail order eradicates many of the normal retail pitfalls: when the clothes arrive, you can examine them closely, ensure that they work with your wardrobe. There is also a flexible money-back policy.

ALTERNATIVE DRESSING

Riding habits

Of all forms of sportswear, equestrian style is by far the most flattering, and the easiest to adapt. There are two distinct types—the everyday outdoor look, with tweedy hacking jacket, twill jodhpurs and leather boots, and the more formal and immaculately groomed dressage style, consisting of glossy top hat, silk cravat, velvet lapels and pristine white jodhpurs.

The tweed or checked hacking jacket is the most accessible piece of the horsewoman's wardrobe. A solid, classic shape—tightly fitting at the shoulder and torso, buttoned to the waist and flaring from the hip—the only drawback in buying an original being that they are moulded like men's (therefore inflexible at the front), and, because they are designed to be showerproof, tend to be lined in cheap cloth. The original riding mac is virtually indistinguishable, minus the status label, from designer versions. Nothing can surpass the cut of genuine jodhpurs. What sets them apart from leggings is that the seams are positioned at

Left *What the well-groomed horsewoman has in her wardrobe could work for you. Dressage style is a cross-fertilisation of practicality, tradition and elegance.*

precise angles to give ease and extra strength where they are needed. Genuine stretch twill jodhpurs now come in a variety of colours from creamy shades, through to brown, black and blue. (The only concession to technology is a hidden square of velcro to fasten at the ankle.) Traditionally shaped jodhpurs (semi-circular on the outside) are only suitable if you have the kind of hips that can accommodate extra curve from knee to hip. Note the optional extras: suede inner patches, and button-up legs. Original cord land army jodhpurs from surplus stores have the same proportions but are made from chunky taupe corduroy with lace-up legs and a deep utility-style seat.

The leather riding boot is a permanent part of any classic footwear collection. Choose what you won't find on the High Street. Rubberised knee-length riding boots are a smart alternative when you don't want to expose your expensive leather boots to adverse weather conditions. There are two types of jodhpur boot—elasticated and buckled. Originals from a saddlery store are around the same price but often superior to their chain-store equivalent because they are made in extra tough leather. Female versions of the man's polo boot—sturdy and distinctive in thick tan leather with lace-up shoe or zipped legs and buckled calf belts—can be bought or ordered from the best saddlery stores. Jockey boots (two-tone with tan tops) are difficult to adapt because they are featherweight and have wafer-thin soles.

Dressage is the most elegant form of equestrian dressing. Genuine dressage jackets, although superbly cut, are heavy and restrictive in practice. Taken out of context, tail coat, silk stock, tie pin and glossy top hat (try it with tulle draped across the brim) add a new dimension to evening wear.

Below *Equestrian dressing in the best tradition where the jodpurs are button front with suede inserts and lace-up polo boots.*

Sporting life

Sportswear is not only the biggest, but the most recurring of all fashion themes. Of these the designers' favourite is sailing—partly because navy and white never seem to lose their appeal, but also because there is the perennial association between seafaring and crisp fresh clothes. Specialist sailing shops, although not cheap, are still inexpensive compared to designer counterparts. Try them for authentic blue and white striped Breton T-shirts, chunky navy sweaters, peaked sailors' caps in cotton or felt (always choose one with minimum detail on it) and traditional sou'westers, oilskins and waterproof trousers. Sailing insignia—whistles, flags, holdalls, and badges—are optional.

In cricket and golf wear, reject contemporary styles (in particular the embroidered sweaters and checked trousers that are strictly for the fairway). Think slightly retro. Both pursuits enjoyed their heyday circa 1930. The cricket look—cream flannel trousers, striped blazer, peaked cap. The golfing wardrobe—traditional Argyll knitted sweater, socks, prickly tweed plus fours, fringed co-respondent brogues in tan and cream.

Of the country pursuits—fishing, hunting and shooting—the accessories are the stars. Try canvas satchels with webbing straps, wicker fishing baskets and interesting walking sticks. Rustic clothes—tweed caps, felted hats and moleskin or corduroy trousers—although autumnal can be worn in other seasons. The tried-and-tested Barbour, so long as it hasn't been subjected to the rigours of country life, looks good in town. Switching climates, safari outfits, based on khaki and cream coloured cotton, can be adapted, but again, accessories have the greatest potential—experiment with gun belts, bush hats, pouch belts and bags.

Surplus style

Army surplus shops are a great source of inexpensive military uniforms and safari clothes. Every girl's favourite, khaki shorts, are great for holidays, belted in with a wide leather belt, and plain white T-shirt. Or try safari-style jackets, parkas and survival gear. On military jackets, the plainer the better (remember if you want to take braiding off it could leave a mark), and because they are made for men, don't expect a perfect fit. The greatest quandary is knowing which size will work—you will have to use your instinct in judging the size by look alone.

Surplus style extends beyond army and navy suppliers—try trade stores—which have the advantage of being extremely cheap because their stock is made in bulk. The most versatile pieces are chefs' checked trousers (brilliant for summerwear belted tightly at the waist, cropped or rolled up with plimsols), waiters' jackets, white or navy cotton drill boilersuits and tough but warm woolly workmen's shirts and jackets.

Above *Fresh, airy sea-faring pieces look just as good on land.*

Let's dance

It only seems like yesterday we were working out, wearing leg warmers to work, and grooving in fluorescent leotards. Fitness and fashion are now so closely bonded that it is difficult to distinguish between what has been bought in a dance or department store. Leotards and leggings are available everywhere so only make a trip to specialist dance suppliers if you want to be a prima ballerina. The prettiest dance shoe of all, the ballet pump, is an exercise in perfect proportions—plain low cut flat shoe in soft leather (black or white) or pastel satin, sometimes with a tiny

Right *Surplus elements taken out of context and used to counterpoint the luxury of a sequinned evening dress.*

Above *With a little imagination, prima ballerina pieces can be transformed into party wear.*

bow at the front. Also try different types of dancing shoes—the highlander, with criss-cross lacing, jazz or Cuban-heeled tap shoes (which can be ordered from some dance shops without the metal toe cap), with eyelet holes to slot a ribbon through.

The ballerina's wardrobe has two facets: ethereal and practical. The soft wool crossover cardigan, slipped on after a day's practice at the barre, is a flattering knitwear shape, and the ballerina-length chiffon skirt has found its way into the non-dancer's wardrobe. Real exercise tights are tough and hold you in far better than anything on the High Street.

Girls will be boys

When Inès de la Fressange, designer and former Chanel house model, was invited to an anniversary party to honour one of the top designers, she had the world's haute couture at her disposal, but pulled on her husband's tuxedo instead. The decision had nothing to do with fashion—androgyny periodically slips in and out of favour. She was demonstrating what women have always known: wearing men's clothes is not only comfortable, but nothing looks sexier on a girl.

Most of us get hooked on androgyny by raiding men's wardrobes and finding that the quality they take for granted is sadly lacking in mainstream women's wear. You start with the shirt - white, striped, turnback or contrast cuffs, or a dinner shirt with turnback cuffs. They are always too large, so the sleeves are rolled back or shortened. The waistcoat presents few problems on fit because it can be pulled in at the back. Men's knitwear is always classic—the cardigan, waistcoat, chunky ribbed sweater. We put a new perspective on men's accessories—the cravat, braces, tie, hat, handkerchief. The singlet (chain stores sell in packs of two) are a cheaper version of the female vest, but make sure the neck depth isn't too low for you. If men's sizes are too big, scour the boys' department, where the shoe section has the kind of walking brogues impossible to find in women's ranges.

There is a world of difference between borrowing and buying. The trick in wearing men's clothes is for them not to look like they belong to someone else: the buttoning—on men left to right—is a surefire giveaway. The Annie Hall look (where the figure is submerged in layers of oversized clothes) is unflattering for most women. It's far better to select one or two items—to retain an element of femininity.

Above *Stockbroker style switches halfway into an airy skirt.*

School's out

School uniforms are only appealing from a distance of about 10 years. Even then, the colours we associate with our blazers are likely to haunt us for ever. The great advantage is price and durability. These clothes are designed to survive the rigours of the school playground, games lessons and all kinds of weather. The traditional flannel blazer, particularly boy's, is brilliant (often unlined but bound at the edges), sometimes has a piped outline. School knitwear (traditionally navy or brown) is often good quality—ribbed V-neck sweaters or cardigans. For girls, pinafores have great potential, the plainer the better. Opt for pleating and preferably a V-neck (scoops can be cut too high for grown women). School shirts are often inferior quality. Try gym shirts, similar to the Fred Perry classic, with stretch collar and cuffs. Gingham is great for summer cool, light and far more pristine than linen—the best buys here are shirts and skirts, and shifts. School accessories can be fun: school bags—the drawstring sand-shoe bag and satchel—and even the schoolboy cap, if you have a suitably gamine look.

Above *Gangster elements taken to extremes.*

Great Scot

The designer fascination with all things north of the border has been going on for so long we can safely assume it will continue. It may be historical, but tartan always manages to make an annual appearance on the prediction pages. Spot the clan in the Yves Saint Laurent, Ralph Lauren and Vivienne Westwood collections—not always strictly traditional, but still unmistakable. The Scotch House, Liberty and border Scottish shops have great lengths of tartan, which can be slung over a shoulder, draped at the hip, or made into anything from a slit skirt to a winter coat. Mix Scottish paraphernalia from furry mohair wraps, scarves, luxurious knitwear and traditional kilts, which last for ever, to the Highland accessories, such as thistle brooches, kilt pins.

Antique clothes show

Remember the magical days spent rummaging through your mother's dressing-up box? Sadly, the childhood appeal of second-hand clothes diminishes in adolescence, returns briefly during college days (on a grant, they are the only kind of clothes you can afford), and adulthood signals the point of no return. We lose sight of the joys of experimentation and succumb to the convenience of pre-packed style. Wearing second-hand clothes may be cheap, but it's hard to do successfully—the buying and particularly wearing of them is an art. Overdose, and you could double up as a Merchant/Ivory film extra. Think carefully about which eras you mix—pair a utility coat with sci-fi silver and you are heading for disaster. The key is balance and subtlety.

The pluses: antique clothes are unique—there is no chance of coming face to face with anyone in the same outfit. They are beautifully made, the cloth is exquisite (in today's technological textile there is little room for craftsmanship) and the cut of clothes (pre-1950s) a form of fine art. You will find beadwork and embroidery that is otherwise impossible to possess unless you have a bank balance large enough to support a haute couture habit. Choose only the best accessories—gloves, silk stockings, jet jewellery and particularly wonderful scarves and stoles.

The minuses: the earlier the garment, the less wear you will get out of it. Many antique clothes, in spite of being made out of fabric that has stood many years of wear and tear, can still be fragile. There are some problems with sizing—the average woman was much smaller and curvier than her modern counterpart, therefore if you are around 5′ 10″, you may find the waist level reaches to underarm. Armholes, too, were generally much smaller. Fastenings, especially hooks and eyes (1920s and 30s)

and zips (1940s onwards) may have gone rusty and need re-placing. Many antique garments were home made and therefore in need of repair especially in the areas where they have been hand finished (around the neck edge, at the hem). Play safe with proportion—avoid telltale exaggerated shoulderlines, only buy hourglass shapes if your figure suits them and bias-cut dresses if you are slim enough for them to glide over your body.

Be equally discriminating about where you look. Make a point of finding out where interesting shops are if you are planning a visit to a new town—the most out-of-the-way places have the best bargains. In your home town, initially try the obvious sources—second-hand charity shops, jumble and nearly new sales (which are slightly more up-market). Also find out where the bric-à-brac and antique shops are (many are tucked away out of view because of low overheads). It is a good idea to get to know the owners—if you express a preference for a particular kind of garment or era they will often keep it aside.

Left Antique clothes are unique in every respect, but particularly in the way they are constructed, the kind of fabric used and the impeccable attention to detail.

SECOND-HAND MODES

'It is an eccentric way of buying clothes, celebrating the fact that you are an individual—it gives total freedom to dress how you like without the constraints of the mass market. They are your own couture ideas for a song. Head-to-toe second hand looks old; the modernity is to have something new underneath and throw a beautiful antique cape on top.'
Isabella Blow,
Features Associate,
British *Vogue*

'I sometimes use antique clothes for inspiration—taking a collar shape and adapting it in my design. I always look for beautifully positioned seams—antique clothes are very body conscious because the absence of stretch means they were constructed in a much more subtle way. The further back you go, the more you are aware of the presence of the body.'
Bella Freud, Designer

'I try to buy the kind of workmanship you can't find now—a beaded tank that could pass for a Versace. Take the clothes out of their historical and social context by adapting them. If you come across a dress with fluted sleeves make it into a skirt. Be very discriminating about what you buy and how you wear it—be very careful not to end up looking like a waif or a second-hand granny.'
Lucinda Chambers,
Fashion Director,
British *Vogue*

'It's the fascination of the past, security, and the lure of romanticism that attracts me to antique clothes. It's a very heavy personality look. Some of the most relaxed and interesting women I know have adopted that image. It is what real people put together—absolutely nothing to do with designers.'
Helen Storey,
Designer

WHAT MAKES A GREAT GARMENT?

Face it: few clothes live up to our expectations. With fashion gurus as our guide, we put faith in our instincts and pray our choices will be eternal. But analyse the evidence: your wardrobe. Now is the time for all great garments to stand up and be counted. How many have stood the test of time? Which ones are beyond redemption? Do any instil the feel-good factor? The most wearable, wantable elements of any wardrobe are easy to spot because they rarely hang in there. They are far too busy being worn, cosseted, prompting compliments, doing time in the dry cleaners or on the washing line. Constant clothes are not necessarily classic—simply the parts of fashion that refuse to be a passing fancy, always managing to fall apart before they fall out of favour. Think back to the point of sale. Chances are the chemistry was instantaneous—today it's still a great good buy.

Left *Great clothes look beautiful, feel wonderful and perform to order. Here, Giorgio Armani's supreme example of simplicity.*

We all know how difficult it is to compile a wardrobe that scores full points on looking immaculate, feeling fine, and toeing the line on demand. Having to buy within a limited budget imposes immediate restrictions, but has no bearing on whether our purchases are destined to be long lasting. Astronomical amounts do not come with a guarantee of continuous wear or eternal satisfaction. Apart from the way it affects the standard of quality, cost is immaterial. There is no fail-safe guarantee of successes: even having a garment made to measure, when you choose the cloth, specify the cut, dictate the detailing, can still add up to an unwearable conclusion.

Clothes are a complex, expensive, and highly emotive issue. Like it or not, they are an important part of our lives. What you choose to wear has the power to make or break your day by influencing your mood, the way you move, and determining whether you face the world as a walking fashion disaster. Demystifying dress codes is only possible with the confidence that knowledge brings. Let's get back to basics. If you are consciously aware that all clothes—from the cheapest to the heights of haute couture—are based on the same structure (and you know what to realistically expect in each category), then you are halfway to fashion heaven. The four prime building blocks are clear—proportion, cut, quality, cloth. Performance is factor X, the aftereffect of putting your wardrobe through its paces.

It is not enough to fully understand clothes. The key to finding great garments is to know yourself. Be brutally honest, even if it hurts. Make a frank assessment of your figure, without falling into the trap of underestimation. We all have parts worth showing off. Develop a talent for fashion flattery by emphasising the good, toning down the bad. Major mistakes are made when we aspire to images that don't take into account our personal needs and appearance. Trying to be fashionable doesn't work. Doing what comes naturally does. The illusion of effortlessness, even if it has in fact been thoroughly contrived, is the most skilful fashion trick in the book.

PROPORTION

Proportion is the tool fashion uses to put a new perspective on clothes. It rings the changes, writes the rules, has the power to date and update. Take a quick flick through *Vogue*'s prediction pages over any five-year timespan and watch the shoulderline widen and narrow, the hemlines rise and fall, the silhouette switch from a triangle to tube. Sandwiched between the extremes

Below *The look that says it all: immaculate cut, consummate quality and finer points finished to perfection.*

Left *Proportion has the power to create illusions and put emphasis on specific areas. A shapely mermaid skirt shows the effect on the silhouette when the designer experiments with fit and flare.*

you will find the classics—neutral shoulderline, knee-level hemline—constant dimensions that circle mainstream fashion. On the flip side, proportion is responsible for memorable fashion gaffes (remember the puffball?), amusing at that moment, but eternally unflattering and only remotely passable on the body beautiful.

At its most basic, proportion is the movement in shoulder or hemline. On a higher level—and more pertinent to the individual—it is a jigsaw of pieces, where each garment, every accessory slots in with and complements the other. In layman's terms, that means the length of a jacket in relation to the skirt, height of a heel to the width of trousers, the dimensions of a coat with the body beneath. But the key to understanding and interpreting proportion is to view it from two angles—what's happening in fashion, and what suits you.

Proportion works on the same principle as make-up. In the same way we highlight our cheekbones, define our eyes, elongate our eyebrows, clothes create cosmetic effects by accentuating and enhancing our natural framework. But it is easy to get stuck in a groove. Apply the same shade of ruby lipstick, or foundation tone year in year out and your face will eventually outlive the look. Equally, the proportions we choose should be periodically reworked. The only solution to shaking off stale ideas is to confront the issue head on. Look at yourself in a full length mirror and adopt an analytical approach. What shape are you? Despite the fact that you probably fall somewhere within the standard-

Watch what happens when lines of black and white are reworked in different combinations.

From left to right

1 *Bold borderlines emphasise an unusual cut.*

2 *Horizontal stripes are notoriously difficult to wear because of their tendency to widen. Note here how black dominates white.*

3 *Stripes strategically positioned emphasise an inventive cut and echo the slit skirt.*

4 *Ticking stripes accentuate the shape of a cropped coat.*

ised size range, 'average' doesn't actually exist. Part of the reason why mass-market fashion sometimes misses the mark on fit is that the idiosyncrasies of the individual anatomy—a long neck, short arms, wide shoulders, slim torso—are so variable that it would be impossible to cater for every combination.

The rules of proportion are dictated by your shape. Generally, though, enhancing specific parts of the figure is easy – at any opportunity flaunt your assets by framing, revealing, making them focal points. Concealing is more complex and can seem contradictory. For example, a rounded physique will often look worse drowned in loose layers and will benefit from a more fitted look. Start by sifting through your wardrobe, experiment, play with shapes, vary the levels, always bearing in mind that the height of a shoe makes a world of difference. Be aware of the basic rules—light illuminates, dark detracts, horizontal stripes widen, vertical ones elongate.

CUT

Cut is the curve, the line, the fit of fashion. Precision scissorwork puts seamlines in flattering positions, picks points where fit and flare excel, draws a shapely neckline, dictates the angle of a sleeve, adds intrigue to a plain surface and always demonstrates an innate understanding of the body.

Incompetent cutting stands out. At first glance odd and disjointed, the badly cut garment is unpleasing to the eye and

Below *Getting proportions right is extremely tricky in tailoring because there are so many elements to consider. The depth of a cuff, width of a collar, angle of a pocket flap are crucial to its success.*

Above Silhouetted on bare skin, precise cutting reveals and conceals parts of the body.

Right Combining inventive seaming with clever cutting – Thierry Mugler's futuristic corset in close-up shows a discerning eye for detail.

uncomfortable to wear because it creates stress points in the wrong places—too loose in the parts that need fit, too tight in the areas where ease is required (around the arm on a jacket, from waist to hip on trousers), each section is off balance.

Measurement is fundamental to cut. The dimensions of design are determined by a designer's basic block, a unique template from which all patterns are drawn. Sizing is relative and therefore impossible to generalise, but as a general rule, the higher the price point, the more generous the cut. Chains targeting the teen and early twenties market, adapt their patterns accordingly, scaling down to fit the adolescent figure. Classic companies, whose target age range is older, cut their shapes slightly more full, more generously around the waist and hip.

Incisions perform tricks, particularly in the art of revealing and concealing. Consider for example, the case of the long narrow skirt, which is tubular in shape and makes you hobble when you walk. Add a thigh-high slit and the skirt becomes an exercise in ease and sexuality. Geometric and curvy cut-outs, at the back, at the neck, create patterns silhouetted on skin.

CLOTH

Cloth holds the key to what a garment can and cannot do, how long it will last, if the cost is justified, and whether it is likely to be well behaved. The characteristics of different types of fabric— unless you are a dressmaker—are difficult to gauge because expectation is founded on guesswork. The chances are you have had sufficient experience of natural fabrics—wool, silk, cotton—to know that they are reliable and reasonably predictable. You understand that wool, depending on the weight, can be warm or cool; silk has versatility that enables it to transform from a taffeta to a chiffon; and cotton is the crispest, coolest fabric around. Recently, you have become accustomed to the properties of Lycra, marvelling at how it magically holds you in and enables the sheerest hosiery to cling without wrinkling at the ankle. Synthetics, you are aware, vary wildly in appearance, the way they are treated, and never let our bodies breath naturally.

Although the traditional textiles remain, technology is advancing rapidly, flooding the marketplace with experimental mixes of yarns and inventive finishes. Today there are so many confusing combinations that often our instinct is the only thing we can rely on when faced with an unrecognisable name. Designers tend to forget what cloth is capable of. As a customer, make sure the fabric suits the purpose, and watch out for mis-

Above left *Voluminous fabrics – particularly lightweight jersey and silk – demonstrate their fluid properties in movement.*

Above right *Lavishly beaded, embroidered or printed, ornamental fabrics reflect the light and add interest to a plain surface.*

Far right *Exquisite quality where every detail – from precision stitching to carefully considered seaming – is clearly visible.*

matches—a winter coat where the weave is far too flimsy and loose to be either practical or protective, the fitted jacket destined to crease (not only where it is unavoidable at the elbow and waist, but anywhere where there is extra pressure), the voluminous skirt where the weight of wool is too heavy to go with the flow. Skimping on cloth cuts costs for the designer, but causes insurmountable problems for you. No matter how expertly cut or beautifully constructed, if the fabric is second rate, there is absolutely no way the garment will ever look first class.

QUALITY

Our perception of quality is subject to personal experience. The chain-store customer expects takeaway fashion at an affordable price, often not stopping to consider if the piece has been professionally finished, or caring whether it dismantles in a couple of seasons. The designer customer takes quality as a matter of course—this is, after all top priority and what she is paying for. Confusion arises because although we know top quality costs, it cannot always be seen. But scrutinise a designer and chain-store collection side by side and the hallmarks of quality become clear: good cloth, elegant buttons, excellent finish, a smooth, carefully pressed appearance.

The finer points of quality are subtle and hard to spot. Put clothes under the microscope. Look inside at the lining—is it good, strong, the right colour, when your jacket flies open, as it inevitably will, do you mind if it is on show? Does it look well pressed? Can you find any puckered seamlines (stitched at breakneck speed, they often slip past quality control)? Is the inside a mass of stray threads (pull one and chances are the seam will unravel)? Is the skirt lined and hem secured to your satisfaction?

Stretch fabrics have become the designer's greatest ally because they hide a multitude of sins. Elastication makes allowances for the less than perfect seam or inaccurate fit. Good tailoring is by far the most difficult thing to fake because it tends to highlight the worst aspects of mass production—pockets (often not put in properly), sleeve heads (gathered because they haven't been eased into shape), cloth (far too susceptible to creasing), buttonholes (finished badly, or even worse, placed in the wrong position, not exactly in line with the buttons). The letdown areas are nearly always where the fastenings are located—look out for zips put in a hurry (their finish matters, even if they're not on show), and buttons, which are liable to be lost through insecure needlework.

Chain stores imitate haute couture, but always bypass the extra time and careful handling to cut costs. Rather than buy simulated craftsmanship, a far better choice is to search for second-hand versions. We rely on our visual senses to assess quality, but feeling them is actually far more important. Tune into the tactile properties of quality by running your fingertips over the fabric.

PERFORMANCE

Ask yourself what you want from your clothes before you invest. Performance is linked to day-to-day life and what is on a garment's agenda must be taken into consideration: does it need to travel well? Do you expect to love it a decade from now? Disillusionment sets in when demands aren't met.

Does the garment suit the purpose? Think practical. There is no point in buying a transparent shirt if you don't like the look of a body underneath, and aren't brave enough to go without. If the coat is full length and you spend most of your day in a car, you will have to deal with superfluous fabric around the leg area. Tailored jackets have a tendency to be inflexible, especially when you need to move swiftly.

A garment's lifespan is also subject to varying expectations. Some parts of a wardrobe are not expected to exist beyond one season—their appeal is due to their association with a fleeting fashion whim and their inexpensiveness.

Never gauge a garment by its hanger appeal. New-born clothes have no life experience. First appearances are deceptive. The initial buzz of buying on looks alone is a sure-fire route to being let down afterwards—that best buy can shrink, fray and re-semble a crumpled tissue only after a few hours' wear.

We fill our wardrobes with clothes that we hope will be ready and willing to rise to the occasion. Yet we usually stick like glue to a small percentage of pieces. That elusive band of great garments holds the key. Look at them. They tell you everything.

Left *Great garments pass the performance test. There is one crucial question to ask an outfit: will it move when you do?*

MAKING IT

Dressmaking is the only option where you call the shots and avoid being at the mercy of manufactured fashion. The decision to start making clothes is sparked by three factors: the first, and most common, stems from a dissatisfaction with what is on the market. The second is the desire or absolute necessity for customised fit. The third is economics—there is no cheaper method of getting the result you want.

Making clothes is one of the most underrated methods of wardrobe building, yet it suffers from an antiquated image as prime time is now filled with more leisurely pursuits. But there are definite fors and againsts. On the plus side, going DIY makes sound economical sense. There is an enormous price difference between off-the-peg and home-made garments, particularly if you take into account the increasing choice and availability of designer patterns. Even at a vastly reduced sale price, a genuine Donna Karan or Karl Lagerfeld is far beyond most women's grasp. Although your version will never be exactly the same, it does enable you to possess a designer label for a fraction of the price. Patterns offer far greater choice on style and flexibility of

MAKING IT: DO'S AND DON'TS

Do

• Start out with the easiest pattern available.

• Arm yourself with the right equipment.

• Test scraps of fabric to make sure you have the right stitch tension.

• Try a dummy run in a similar but cheaper cloth.

• Press as you go—ironing gives a professional finish.

• Look at your existing clothes—these give an indication of the styles that suit and also measurements.

• Invest in a reputable reference book on sewing techniques.

Don't

• Experiment with a shape you have never tried before.

• Select a pattern that is beyond your capabilities, particularly if it involves specialist tailoring techniques.

• Choose fabrics that are difficult to handle (chiffon, velvet and silk jersey) until you have gained more experience.

• Rely on guess work—follow the pattern to the letter.

• Rush it—always allow yourself sufficient time.

• Take shortcuts.

fit—the waist level can be moved up or down, hem and sleeve length adjusted at whim. On the down side, the trouble with home-made clothes is they often look exactly that. Therefore, take extra care particularly with buttonholes, topstitching and pressing. Remember the X factor: in dressmaking there is no guarantee of what the end result will be.

Sewing is easy if you adopt a step-by-step approach, and resist the temptation to run before you can walk. One of the main fears is knowing how or where to start. Sewing classes take the mystique out of making clothes by easing you into handling fabric, cutting out, and understanding the language of patterns. For the absolute novice, start by attending dressmaking classes—your local school may be a good place to begin—or put yourself under the guidance of an experienced seamstress. The Liberty School of Sewing runs courses in everything from building a boned ballgown to making a waistcoat and tie.

Choose your style by using your wardrobe as a guideline. Decide which styles really suit. Is there a specific neckline, fit, fabric that always looks just right? You are working in the dark gauging solely from a drawing or photograph. Shop around, try clothes out, make a mental or, better still, a written note of the way it is made, but be specific. What is the neckline like? Where are the seams positioned? What kind of fabric is used? At the very least, have a rough outline of proportion and shape in mind before you consult the pattern books. These are lined up near the haberdashery section in good department stores and require careful consultation. Pattern books use a combination of illustrations and photographs, and categorise clothes by garment types (blouses, dresses, sportswear), and by complexity. *Vogue* patterns are categorised within one of four sections: Very Easy, Easy, Average and Advanced (which should only be tackled by experts). Colour coding indicates the price of the pattern, and sometimes the intricacy of the pattern pieces. A chart gives a graphic line drawing, and all the information you need to know: a clear description of fit, shape, detail, length, whether it is lined, recommended fabrics and list of 'notions' (extras—e.g. buttons, shoulderpads, zips, etc.). Make sure you are buying the right size—patterns are often more generously proportioned than off-the-peg clothes.

Start with something easy. Trousers with a drawstring or elasticated waistband (no zips or buttons to worry about), a scoop necked shift (that can be pulled effortlessly over the head) or a plain uncomplicated tunic or kimono jacket. As a novice dressmaker, it is unwise and uneconomical to attempt complicated

Below *Novice seamstresses should start with something simple. A sleeveless shift is ideal for beginners because it bypasses all the stumbling blocks – there are no sleeves, collars or tricky finishes to worry about.*

constructions. Stumbling blocks are inevitable, but being over ambitious will put you off for life. Try a dummy run with calico (technically called a toille) if the cloth is expensive. This gives an indication of what the end result will be, if the length is correct, if the waist point is in its proper position.

Choosing the right fabric is critical. Make a note of the recommended types (listed on the back of the pattern). Patterns are made specifically to react favourably to certain types of cloth: a dress that was designed to be made in jersey, will act out of character in anything else. Most department stores have an excellent selection that changes seasonally. Buy thread, shoulder-pads and lining at the same time so that you can match colours and have everything to hand. There are alternative sources too. Mills and manufacturers where factory shops are attached often have sample lengths on sale. A few designers sell end of rolls and remnants. Jean Muir's Turquoise Room, below her studio at 59–61 Farringdon Road, EC1, is a treasure trove of every type of fabric from silk jersey to tweed, suede and a selection of custom-made buttons and buckles.

Dressmaking takes time. Even for the most basic shapes, at the very least allow yourself one day for cutting out, two for sewing and pressing, and one to finish off. This varies wildly of course, but don't expect to rustle up a tunic in a couple of hours. Using the right equipment is important. A good sewing machine (with facilities for buttonholding and overlocking so that you can neaten rough edges), a sharp pair of dressmaking scissors (and smaller ones for snipping stray threads), a tape measure, and adequate space for cutting out (ideally a long smooth, waist-level table) which is far more practical and kinder to your posture than kneeling on the floor, are all must-haves. Lay the cloth correctly, (completely flat, right sides together) place the pattern pieces exactly in accordance with the layout plan provided, making sure the grainline is at exactly the right position. Notches and marks are fundamental guidelines in getting it right, telling you at which point to join the pieces during the sewing process.

Before any serious dressmaking starts, ensure your machine is set on the correct tension by testing scraps of fabric. Follow the instructions to the letter—tack where it tells you to, ease in the sleeves, press as you sew. Never be tempted to take short-cuts.

THE CLASSICS

Can classic appeal be defined? Eternal, understated, wearable, desirable—all words that apply. They are the clothes women want to wear and the world wants to buy. Where fashion is based on innovation, classics avoid radical change. Look at any prediction page. Hot from the catwalk, the classics reappear season after season, but always subtly updated. When focusing on the key trousers, coat, or shade of camel, fashion analysts are not merely restating their popularity—look closer and you will see a gentle development in length, collar shape, proportion. Classics are not immune to fashion—rather they run parallel, their success due to the fact that they are never obviously identifiable with a specific season. But what exactly are they? Basically, they're the core collection of shapes that form the basis for all clothes. True classics are unobtrusive, but never boring.

Left *Proving the point that true classics have the power to stand the test of time: Princess Cyril Troubetskoy photographed in 1946.*

'The contradiction is that
although classics are timeless
there is always a new way of
wearing them at a given time
that is right.'

SARAH MOWER,

FASHION JOURNALIST

Above *The utility look, top to toe—*
the cling-fit twinset, classic turnup
tweed trousers and sturdy lace-up
walking shoes.

British classics, in particular, take their cue from men's wear, some virtually indistinguishable from the real thing. The British are masters at mixing functionality and fashion—our macintoshes, for example, loved world-wide—but also expert at producing top quality tailoring and knitwear. Internationally, there is one basic rule in classic design—avoid exaggeration. This applies to everything—detail, silhouette, even fabric and pattern. Classics neatly bypass the elongated or skimpy shoulderline, wide lapel. This gentle approach even applies to colour: the classic palette is an abbreviated shade range that can be narrowed down to six: navy, black, cream, camel, grey and white. Natural fibres go hand in hand with classics—cotton, cashmere, pure wool, and favourite patterns are those that don't date—herringbone, check, tartans—occasionally scaled up and brightly coloured but always keeping to their traditional blueprint.

The cornerstone of classic dressing is quality. We are now dealing on a level where buying centres on a solid knowledge of clothes. Choosing them raises the perpetual questions of how they will behave, whether they suit, if they will last, but the most pertinent of all—will they date? A razor-sharp instinct helps. It is no coincidence that the most successful classic dressers are usually those whose antennae are trained to detect quality from a hundred yards. But for the uninitiated, the natural starting point is your own wardrobe. Sift out the all-time best buys—the basic shapes that work for you. Scrutinise what is special about each particular piece: it could be as specific as the depth of the belt loop or as general as the colour of a coat. This information will provide the basis for your personal classic template. Buying power is another important consideration: the true test of any classic is its lifespan. Everyone has their own switch-off price point, but the fact is that top-quality timeless clothes inevitably cost more. Psychologically, you may need to justify this on a cost-per-wear basis. Ask yourself: is the jacket likely to soon lose its appeal? Are those trousers adaptable enough to work with your existing wardrobe? Is that white shirt exactly right?

But even armed with a crystal-clear idea of the kind of styles you are looking for, finding them requires forethought. Tried-and-tested hunting grounds on the High Street may have been successful for the seasonal must-haves, but are not necessarily the best place to find a winter coat. One of the main problems is that the High Street fashion philosophy rarely centres on understatement. Here, unless you are on the lookout for a plain pure wool, crew-neck sweater, or cotton T-shirt (two of the top quality basics that are superbly produced by chain stores),

CLASSIC FABRIC GUIDE

You may be familiar with fabric, even *au fait* with texture, but are you tuned into which cloths are genuinely classic? Here, a step-by-step guide to the top seven timeless weaves and wools.

Cashmere

The rarest and most luxurious of all natural fibres, spun from the soft underbelly of the kashmir goat found in Inner Mongolia. Instantly recognisable by its unique finish and luxurious feel, cashmere is often mixed with less expensive yarns (e.g. silk, pure wool) to lower the cost.

Cotton

Soft absorbent fabric, sometimes mercerised to give a lustrous surface. Can be washed frequently without affecting the structure. Adaptable to many kinds of finish from piqué to velvet.

Denim

Traditionally indigo coloured, twill weave fabric in pure cotton, but also available with Lycra content to give extra flexibility. Usually stiff at first, but softens on washing and after regular wear. Extremely strong and durable, denim loses its colour gradually,

fading at crease and stress points (e.g. back of knees). Allow for shrinkage.

Linen

Classic summer fabric with a tendency to crease. Cool and comfortable, linen is also supple, tough and translates into anything from fine lawn to suiting. Plain linens show creasing more easily than patterned, where it is slightly camouflaged. Works very well in voluminous shapes.

Silk

An affordable luxury fabric, loved for its intense colour and high shine. The many variations include organza (slightly transparent), taffeta (crisp—great for sculptured designs),

chiffon (light and airy), crepe de chine (soft with shine), shantung (irregular slub yarns running through) and jersey (fine knitted fabric that drapes and moves beautifully). Washed silk has a slightly chalky finish, and is cared for by hand washing.

Tweed

The traditionals—houndstooth, herringbone, Prince of Wales check—are translated into various sizes and weights. Harris Tweed is one of the most famous, mainly because of its history, but also its unlikely long-running association with designer Vivienne Westwood. It is spun from tough Scottish wools and hand-woven by craftsmen on the Isle of Harris and Lewis; showerproof, extremely strong, with a slightly prickly finish, it is recognisable by its orb trademark.

Wool

One of the most versatile of all classic fabrics, in many different weights and textures from wool crepe to mohair. The development of cool wool has switched the properties of wool from strictly winter to summerweight fabric.

'Timeless, an on-going elegance, something that changes minimally. A true classic is updated with the seasons but still keeps its traditional features.'

SYLVIA HAMMERSLEY,

HEAD OF DESIGN,

AQUASCUTUM

cost-cutting will always be made on cloth before eliminating superfluous detail. Look further afield and venture into unexpected territory—equestrian outfitters, for example, are an obvious but often by-passed place to buy a traditional riding mac. Many British traditionalists—Aquascutum, Windsmoor, Burberrys, for example—all excellent sources of classic clothes, often suffer, unfairly, from a middle-aged image that can spark instant turn-off for anyone under thirty. In reality their shops are frequented by young highly discriminating Japanese, American and French shoppers—export figures alone, show an international appreciation of English craftsmanship. Jayne Pickering, British *Vogue*'s Fashion Editor who selects and styles clothes for the 'Dash Cash' pages, scours these stores every season: 'I always find something that women would want for their wardrobes—very classic wool trousers, a navy pea coat. They are great for finding less expensive versions of classics that designers are doing on the catwalk. I look for something that is well-cut, simple—a good, basic essential. They are undoubtedly the best place to find those things.' In short, ignore the periphery of fashion packaging. When it comes to classic dressing it's the clothes that count.

FINER DETAILS

If your bank balance won't stretch to investment, take heart. Traditional touches guarantee a classic dimension without costing the earth. Swapping shiny plastic buttons for real horn, wearing a beret with a trouser suit or stitching an embroidered club badge on your blazer pocket may seem tiny steps to take, but they will make a world of difference.

Buttoning
Authentic horn (tiny shirt to chunky toggle), jet (glossy black often with graphic incisions), plaited leather, mother of pearl, and gilt sailor-style with anchors and sailing motifs. Chain clasps and hooks (often used to close wraps and jackets). All available from haberdashery and antique button specialists.

Insignia
Strictly traditional school, sailor, club-house badges in enamel or pocket-sized embroideries to wear on a navy blazer. Braids (knitted and woven) Chanel-style paired with tweed. Monogrammed shirt pockets.

Gentlemen's Wardrobe
The finer details—cufflinks, braces, cravats, ties, tie pins, collar studs, silk handkerchief —look great on a woman.

Accessories
Hats: beret, straw coolie, panama, boater, bowler, top hat, trilby, deerstalker. Scarves: anything polka dotted or with a signature print. Belts: woven leather, saddle stitched, or plain. Bags: satchel, Kelly, briefcase. Shoes: brogue, ballet pump. Boots: jodhpur and riding boot.

THE COAT

'Generous sizing is very important. Not too big, but always large enough to wear over a jacket. The coat should be simple—any variation on double breasted, or what we call a polo coat which has a fly front so that the buttons are covered gives a very clean look. Choose a classic colour—rich camel, navy or black, and good natural fabric—cashmere, camelhair or pure wool. The lining needs to be substantial. It is always the first part of the coat to wear out.'

CELIA FARMER, DEPUTY PRESS OFFICER, JAEGER

Traditionally the biggest investment in any woman's wardrobe, the coat's lifespan is always measured in years, never seasons. Because it is expected to perform annually (and intensively, every day for approximately four to six months) not only must it be physically tough, but also adaptable enough to interact with an ever-changing range of winter clothes. The prime consideration when buying a coat is lifestyle. You should have a clear idea of where it will be worn, and how it should look. Ask specific questions: do you need a city coat where smartness is the prime consideration or an easy cover-up to and from the office? Will you be wearing it in a car (shorter is always more practical)? Is appearance secondary to its flair for keeping out the cold? The answers to these elementary questions will give a basic outline of the kind of coat you are looking for. Sometimes trusting first instincts can mean the unexpected turns out to be an all-time best buy. Anna Harvey, British *Vogue*'s Deputy Editor remembers 'a blonde cashmere coat that I bought about ten or twelve years ago and still to this day pull out of the wardrobe on a winter's day. It's the most amazing coat—a lovely shape, and has never dated. It's a trench, tie belt, very worn now around the cuffs, the colour is totally impractical, gets filthy instantly, but it's just such a beautiful coat and an absolute pleasure to wear.'

Ask any designer, from the High Street to Savile Row, and there will be a unanimous answer when asked to identify the most important part of the coat—it is always the cloth. Unlike the jacket, skirt, or trousers, where flaws can be easily disguised because the fabric is sliced into smaller sections, inferior material in a coat has nowhere to hide. Its dimensions mean that an uninterrupted length is constantly on view. Functional requirements decided, next come colour and texture. A definite decision on whether it should be dark, light, textured, patterned or plain will cut down search time by focusing the eye on what is relevant.

Below *Taking its cue from military styling, the gilt button becomes a focal point on the double-breasted wool overcoat.*

Look in your wardrobe—the coat must mix with other pieces. For this reason, camel is popular because it has a neutral quality, enhances most colours, and is complimentary to any skin tone.

Deciding where to buy is as crucial as knowing what to look for. Rule one: economies cannot be made on the coat. Cutting corners will mean that although the coat may have a classic exterior, its structure will not last. The first winter coats of the year are in store (around August) at the height of the holiday season—at a time when the suntan has yet to fade and the mind isn't tuned into wintry weather. But this is the best moment, when stocks are at their optimum, to buy. The most common mistake occurs when winter coats are tried on over thin summerweight clothes. Put into practice, the coat will probably be too tight when worn with winterweight layers. Too skimpy and it will destroy the fit by putting strain on the front fastening, too loose and it may be inclined to slide backwards over the shoulders. Aim for a shape that will comfortably ease over your existing clothes.

Style is next on the agenda. Assessing the look of a coat by standing immobile in front of a mirror gives a false impression of how it will work in everyday life. Because coats are made for walking the best look good in movement. As a general rule, volume looks appealing, particularly in softer, plusher cloths. Until recently, extra width equalled extra heaviness. Newer blends have solved that problem, in weaves that successfully balance warmth and weight. Few coats fit perfectly—the key difficulties usually being sleeve and hem length. Alterations are notoriously difficult to tackle yourself; ask if there is a seamstress service in store at the time of buying and arrange for any lengthening or shortening to be dealt with on the spot.

Functional design details—tags to close the collar at the neck, button-down pockets, detachable hoods, tie belts—all add extra cost to your coat. Therefore, choose these only if they will be used. Pockets are an essential feature of the classic coat, and the position of them crucial, ideally at the right level and angle. The collar should complement, never dominate, but fit in with the shoulderline, and overall proportion of the coat. Finer details count. Look inside and make sure the loop for hanging the coat is strong enough to take the strain. Extra buttons must be provided as these will be impossible to obtain later. The type and number of fastenings are important. Coats are taken off and put on regularly throughout the day, therefore multiple buttons will only result in extra time. Likewise belts—if you don't need one, do without, particularly if it has a heavy buckle that is designed to be an eye-catching centrepiece, not hanging at the side.

Left *The ultimate classic coat is uncomplicated, understated with detail that never dates.*

COAT: KEY POINTS

● Think years, not seasons, ahead.

● Good cloth and lining are equally important.

● Horn buttons are the best quality.

● Choose fabric carefully— remember cashmere may be the most luxurious but not the most hard wearing.

● Select a base colour. The three key tones are camel, black and navy.

THE JACKET

'Jackets cover up and accentuate parts of the body. That basic idea works for all women. Jackets need to be structured yet comfortable, but also very strong. To justify the price there should be something special about it—that could mean use of colour, a great button, but it must also have points of quality—very good linings, an inside pocket—small details that look like they have had a lot of love spent on them.'

ARABELLA POLLEN, DESIGNER

For decades the jacket was worn exclusively as part of a suit or in place of a coat; today it has a new role—as office armour. We demand far more of the modern jacket, because it is now expected to perform in everyday life, the most desirable combines the definition of tailoring with the comfort of a cardigan.

What makes a jacket classic? Take the eternal appeal of a man's—well-cut lapels, traditional tailoring, nicely positioned buttons, uncreasable fabric, Savile Row finish—and add a feminised silhouette. But what are the specific points to watch? First, proportion and fit. Because the classic jacket is one that skims from shoulder to hip level, the cut of it must echo your anatomy. The focal point is the lapel, selected because it instinctively appeals to the eye. Choose a neutral-sized shoulder - neither too narrow nor too wide. Like the ever-changing hemline, this is the first part of the jacket to reflect fashion. Make sure the shoulder pad is secured in the correct position (just touching the tip of the sleeve head) and not too deep (nothing looks worse than a jacket hovering above your natural shoulderline). For versatile length, choose hip level, which gives sufficient coverage and is adaptable to the trouser, and the knee- and full-length skirt.

Secondly, examine for ease. The most common criticism of the jacket is that its streamlined shape limits movement. In most cases, restriction is situated at the armhole—check by circling and bending your arms when trying on. A well-cut jacket allows this without the necessity of a deep set or wide sleeve. View from every angle: a jacket could be perfect at the front, but bag at the back (the cause may be the lining or not fitting naturally at your waist). Does it have a vent? If not, you will have to put up with unbuttoning it every time you want to sit down. Analyse the sleeve angle: ideally sleeves should reflect your posture and fall slightly forward rather than hanging straight down.

Thirdly, scrutinise the fastenings: a single button positioned at the waist creates a clean line while standing, but how does it

Above *Based on traditional men's tailoring, the woman's blazer is subtly reworked, the silhouette curved and any sharp angles emphasised with a wide white borderline.*

Left *Classic women's jackets are firmly rooted in men's wear. Apart from variation in size and shape, all key details remain the same.*

behave when sitting? Unless it is at exactly the right level, the jacket will gape. The waist point must correspond with your own or the fit may be knocked totally off balance when buttoned up.

Finally, study the finer details. Good lining is essential. Top stitching, unless at bespoke level, looks shoddy. Flaps on pockets can be tucked in or out, which is particularly useful for concealing the pocket when it starts to bag. Cuff buttons with buttonholes (as opposed to simply stitched on top) signal extra special attention to detail.

What about cloth? Reject those that crease easily or are susceptible to shine. By and large, natural fabrics are best. Consider their characteristics. A Harris tweed, for example, is not only virtually indestructible but showerproof, too. A pure wool gaberdine will retain its shape. Tweeds or twill (particularly those that are loosely woven with Lycra content) move when you do. Stripes and checks, scaled up or down, are a clever device to define shape or add extra colour but always make sure they match, particularly at the shoulder point.

Even within the classic jacket, there are variations in style. The blazer was originally summer wear, but is now virtually seasonless—lightweight wool gaberdine or linen for summer, and felted or melton wool for winter. Although a close relation to the classic jacket, there are subtle differences between them. Blazers are normally navy, much looser, traditionally double breasted, hip level, and uniformly accessorised with gilt buttons. The blazer has specific ideal partners—wide white linen trousers or a long pleated skirt, and the white or navy plimsoll to keep pace with the seafaring feel.

THE MAC

'A true, top quality mackintosh is 100 per cent waterproof, made out of rubber coated fabric, and seams specially treated: stuck together, stitched, taped on top so that even the stitch holes won't let water in. The more they're worn, the more supple they will become. Mackintoshes are loved primarily because they function, but put it this way, most people who buy a mac are never going to stand out in the rain for four hours—there is just something very appealing about the style.'

ROBIN VEITCH, MANAGING DIRECTOR, TRADITIONAL WEATHERWEAR

It's waterproof, windproof and always improves with age, but the real charm of the macintosh is that it is geared to the British climate. The mac is a design classic on a par with the Morris Minor. Totally functional, every part—from the shape of the sleeve, expert seam treatment, to the special rubberised fabric—has a purpose. It slips over your arm (just in case there's a shower), folds to order and is so light you never know it's there at all. The mac fits easily over your other clothes. It gives more protection than a coat, but there is a limited choice—traditional women's macs are often simply scaled-down versions of men's.

What are the points that distinguish an ordinary from an excellent mac? A great mac grows old gracefully, the rubberised cotton guaranteed to turn supple in time. But this rule only applies to the best macintoshes on the market. At Traditional Weatherwear, in Scotland (who make under their own label, but also produce for Polo Ralph Lauren, Paul Smith, Katharine Hamnett, Calvin Klein and Hermès) superb macs are made by craftsmen, whose expertise centres on a highly skilled method of handling the seams that are sealed, stitched and then taped to make them totally waterproof. Although the best kind of macs are built to last, they must still be treated well. Inside, look out for instructions on how to keep clean (dry cleaning is out—often all they need is a surface scrub, and to be hung up at room temperature to dry naturally). Never be tempted to speed up the process by draping your mac over the nearest radiator.

Although there are around fifteen variations, only two types of mac are typical. The standard classic mac is designed to a traditional specification—it will probably be pale-coloured, with a raglan sleeve (the kind that curves from shoulder to underarm, allowing extra layers underneath), optional belt, a button-fly front, and with eyelet holes dotted under the armhole (essential as rubberised cloth needs to breathe). This pared-down design is counterpointed by the more elaborate style of the equally popular riding mac. It is instantly identifiable by its equestrian fixtures and fittings: leg straps, elasticated inner wind-cuffs to stop the rain running down and the wind blowing through the sleeve, a waist strap so that it stays closed even when the mac is unbuttoned. The proportions: a fan vent at the back (theoretically to keep the seat of the pants protected from the elements) and long enough to span a horseback. This kind of mac—adored by the Italians and the most crucial part of the mounted police uniform—has been adapted at designer level by Ralph Lauren's Polo label, and Gucci.

Most macs are manufactured within a colour range of putty and cream. There is no solid theory for the narrow spectrum, except the basic observation that on rainy days, we want to lighten

'It is style rather than fashion. Classics are pieces that last through time simply because they are a very good design, usually pure, simple and practical.'

MARGARET HOWELL,

DESIGNER

MAC: KEY POINTS

• Length and proportion should be dictated by what you want to wear it with—a cropped A-line shape works over leggings, a full length mac with a long skirt.

• Eyelet holes under the arm are essential in rubberised macs.

• Look for instructions inside on how to keep clean.

• If you want a mac to be seasonless, choose one with a detachable inner lining.

• Try specialist stores, traditional chains and riding outfitters.

up. There are brightly coloured macs on the market, but beware—these shades can fade. Inside, detachable wool linings enable the mac to double up as a winter and spring coat. But what of actual shapes? Remember that rubberised fabric behaves in a totally unique way. Even when it is worn in, rubberised cloth is still fairly crisp, and is more suited to the structured rather than fitted silhouette. The A-line shape—cropped or long—works well. The only way to achieve waist definition in any mac is to actually belt it. Although true macintoshes are those that are water tight, you can find the same design in gaberdine and in staunch traditionalists, like Burberrys, the mac has undergone an image change—turning into a satin trench after dark.

THE SKIRT

'There are two skirt shapes that are constant—the straight knee-length skirt and longer pleated skirt. The most important consideration is fit. Women tend to have a fixation about sticking to a particular size without taking into account any changes in body shape. You should be able to sit down and stand up comfortably. The cause of creasing is regularly blamed on the cloth, but more often than not it is purely because the skirt is just too tight.'

PATRICIA SAXBY, MARKETING CONTROLLER, WINDSMOOR

Does the classic skirt exist? If fashion is assessed by the rise and fall of a hemline surely the notion of classic length is a contradiction in terms. On the catwalk, lengths are an indicator of designer change, but in reality skirt choice is down to one thing: personal preference. Specific lengths say certain things: knee length is fail-safe in the office, long equals ethereal, the split skirt sexuality. Ultimately, which skirt you wear is subject to experimentation, but dictated by body shape and lifestyle.

There are specific types that have stood the test of time. The standard, tailored, slim skirt ending somewhere around the knee with a narrow waistband, double darts and vent at the back is established as the classic, seasonless skirt. It is acceptable executive wear, can be worn at the weekend, and easily translates into chunky tweed (worn with thick knit tights so the legs won't get cold) or lightweight wool (accessorised with sheer tights). To some extent, tailoring has been overtaken by the stretch version of the slim knee-length skirt. From the manufacturers' point of view, this means less cost as often all that is needed are two knee-length pieces of cotton Lycra, side seams and the fabric does the

'You can always pull classic clothes out of the wardrobe and wear them without feeling conscious of being fashionable or unfashionable.'

LIZ THODY,

FASHION STYLIST.

Left *The great British mac built to last in light, supple, waterproof cloth. The basic design remains virtually unchanged from year to year.*

SKIRT: KEY POINTS

• Remember classic skirts are exempt from designer dictates—choose the length that suits.

• Look for lining, even in the lightest skirts.

• Grown-on waistbands (where the skirt is extended to finish above waist level) give a clean line, but waistbands actually stop stretching.

• Use the specified size only as a general guideline—be flexible and buy skirts that fit comfortably.

• Watch your proportions— jacket and skirt shapes must work together.

Right *Hemlines are always first to reflect fashion changes. The classic skirt steers clear of extremes in shape and length.*

rest. For the wearer, the plus is elasticity eliminates bagging; the down side is that stretch skirts have a habit of riding up the leg and always cling rather than skim. The dimensions of the knee-length straight skirt enables it to adapt to longer or shorter jackets, a high or low-heeled shoe. When buying, remember side pockets often cannot work properly if the shape dictates a close fit. As a point of quality in tailoring, always look for lining inside (which will create a smooth line) and a deep hem to allow leeway for lengthening later.

But what about long? Short skirts are fine for women who are content with their legs, but what do you choose if you like to be covered up? An elongated version of the tailored skirt is elegant but impractical and always restrictive unless it has ease. This can take the form of vents, pleats, side-splits or simply a gradual widening of skirt shape. Because it solves the problem of mixing movement with a slim silhouette, the pleated skirt—short or long—is popular. Here, note the type, size and direction of the pleat. These are the subtleties of design that determine how the skirt will behave. In the most uncomplicated version of the pleated skirt (where plain sharp knife pleats fall vertically from the waist), it is important to notice whether pleats free-fall from the waistband (this will mean the slightest body curve will be echoed in the outline), or if they are stitched down to hip level (generally much more flattering as they hold the pleats in where it matters). Designers use the position and type of pleat to direct flare where they want it to be: all-round pleating to give circular flare, box pleats and kick pleats channel extra ease to specific areas. The kilt—flat at the front and flaring around the body— combines pleat with tailoring techniques and looks great short or long. Traditional tartans can be contemporary, but plain colours work equally well. What if you want to combine length with leg? A wrap skirt is the obvious answer, but unless perfectly constructed tends to reveal more than it conceals.

The skirt, like the jacket, is one of the key garments in the wardrobe. The same colour code applies: base shades of black, navy and grey are likely to be the most worn. Colour affects proportion: a light long skirt will focus attention on the lower half of the body, dark tones detract. Patterns, particularly bold checks and wide stripes, are difficult to get right and normally attractive only when abbreviated. The use of evening fabrics—for example, a short skirt in velvet, or long pleated in a fine silk chiffon—translates tried-and-tested classic shapes from day to night, and, although virtually unchanged from season to season, give the impression of being totally new.

Right *Crisp linen trousers that meet the exacting criteria of comfortable fit, with minimal detail and optional turnups.*

TROUSERS

'The best trousers are slim cut, well-fitting, with one pleat for a more narrow line, and always belted at the waist. Jodhpurs, especially in cavalry twill, are great but the exaggerated shape doesn't suit everyone. In time, leggings will become a classic, simply because we're hooked on the comfort of them. But I'm talking about the ones that are cut like ski pants - not the kind that get mistaken for tights.'

MARGARET HOWELL, DESIGNER

Trousers are often the most difficult item of clothing to find. Because they have a three-point fit criteria—comfortable at the waist, sufficient room to move and leg length keeping pace with your anatomy—their cut must reflect your form. Enter leggings—the best-selling invention that came out of the Lycra revolution. For many women it answered their prayers for one-size leg coverage and what to wear with a longer jacket. One drawback: they have a tendency to act like a second skin. For fail-safe flattery, classic, tailored trousers—usually with knife crease front, side pockets, front pleat and double darts at the back for good fit—are a design that has never been surpassed.

To create the right effect, classic trousers must be well-proportioned—not too tight, shaped or cropped. They are eternally complimentary because they skim the hips and suggest a line over the leg. Length is important—this will determine how the trousers will fall, but the exact fit is down to you. Your figure-type may suit a looser proportion, your legs possibly long enough for turnups (they tend to foreshorten), your waist narrow so a more generous size can be gathered in with a wide belt. On discovering a particular designer or label that fits you perfectly, stick with it. Sizing varies considerably in trouser shapes and that basic block—unique to each individual designer—will remain constant season after season, adapting only to accommodate extra pockets and variations in fabric.

A classic look can be translated through the seasons. For winter, wool twill or flannel are flexible and warm enough, preferably half-lined front and back to prevent bagging. Make sure the cloth isn't too stiff—a wider trouser needs a certain measure of fluidity to work correctly. Coarser fabrics should be fully lined to stop the cloth from irritating the skin. Linen, the only fibre that is acceptably creasable, is great for summer but often too transparent to be suitable for slender trousers, and performs much better in a wider proportion.

TROUSERS: KEY POINTS

● Remember sizing varies considerably between designers.

● Turnups are impossible to alter at home—choose only if the trousers are the correct length.

● Belt loops are essential and should be wide or narrow enough to accommodate your existing accessories.

● Choose flexible, uncreasable cloths. Linen is the only exception.

● Make sure trousers are comfortable enough to sit as well as stand in.

When buying trousers, you should examine them inside and out. Look for lining that corresponds with the season and type of cloth. The logic behind this is not only to allow the trousers to fall correctly but to strengthen stress points. Pocket bags should be secured at the side seam for added reinforcement. On the outside, jetted pockets (the kind that look like a random slit the width of a hand-span) are not as strong as a diagonal or straight pocket that has the added security of being sewn into both waistband and the side. Belt loops are essential — nothing looks better than a good quality leather belt slotted through. This will also keep the trousers positioned at the right level (a must if the waistband is too large). Unless trousers are a perfect length, avoid turnups — these are extremely difficult to alter and should only be tackled by an experienced seamstress.

The final effect of classic trousers can be enhanced — or destroyed — by adding the wrong accessory. As a general rule, plain is best. In footwear a flat leather brogue, suede loafer, or low heeled sandal will give a strong base for classic trousers. With linen, a clean white or navy plimsoll, with or without laces, always looks good. Belts can be woven (often a more casual effect) or in a rich bridle leather with a solid brass or silver buckle. On top, what you wear, and how you wear it, is important. Any excess fabric from a shirt or sweater slipped inside will inevitably create problems in achieving a smooth fit. To counteract this, try any variation on a body, a vest or a great white shirt, its tails pulled to the front and secured in a tight crisp knot.

THE TROUSER SUIT

'Today's trouser suit is shapely — it's got waist definition, a softer shoulderline, gentler body shape, and doesn't look like you've borrowed your boyfriend's. The ideal trouser suit is something you update every season and is endlessly versatile — slip on a rollneck and it's leisure wear, smarten up with a silk shirt, change your earrings and you can go to dinner in it.'

BETTY JACKSON, DESIGNER

Until conventional dress codes totally relax, it's debatable whether the trouser suit will ever replace the skirt suit. But in the meantime, it is fashion's greatest solution to the eternal dilemma of combining smartness with comfort. The trouser suit is fast, eliminating experiments on finding two pieces that will work together within your wardrobe, and at the same time making hosiery and shoe choice easy. It is practical. The skirt and jacket—

Above *Adapting to a hot climate, the summer trouser suit evolves into something light, loose and cool.*

Left *Great trouser suits are about balance. The jacket and trousers must be equally desirable and be able to work together and apart.*

'Simple style, neutral colour, great fabric, cut and finish.'

CELIA FARMER,

DEPUTY PRESS OFFICER,

JAEGER

TROUSER SUIT: KEY POINTS

- Identify the kind of jacket and trouser shape that suits you best before buying.

- Keep it plain—trouser suits should be a base to work from.

- Ask questions. Is it versatile? Do you like both pieces equally?

- Aim for a curvy, in preference to a masculine outline.

- City suits on women only work if they're worn with a sense of humour.

even in the most flexible fabrics—will always be more restricting. The trouser suit signals contemporary thinking and in the right shape, and with the right attitude, is far sexier than a skirt suit.

Great classic trouser suits should combine the best elements of the styles that suit in both trousers and jacket. Ultimately it is a balance of two pieces that combine ease and elegance, never with one garment overriding the other. Finding a perfect pair of trousers or jacket as separate items is difficult - but the trouser suit raises a unique set of questions. The most obvious of these is in fit. Few women require the same size top and bottom, and as the trouser suit is designed and purchased as a pair, the problems are plain. Let's assume your body is sufficiently symmetrical— what exactly should you look for? First, bear in mind that the jacket and trousers must have equal appeal. Unless both are exactly right, don't buy. If in doubt, look elsewhere for separate garments that complement, but don't necessarily match each other. The attraction of the trouser suit is that it is a complete look—with the bonus of being able to be worn apart. But constant preference to one piece, aside from being financially impractical, can lead to discrepancies in colouration (due to extra dry cleaning) and an imbalance in wear and tear.

Today's classic trouser suit fuses the best elements of men's tailoring—immaculate fabric and finish—with a feminised cut. Masculine detail and sharp shapes should be avoided. Equally, avoid fussy details. A draped collar may be utilised by some designers as a way of crossing the borderline between masculinity and femininity, but the most wearable are those that offer a simple, solid base for dressing up. The jacket should be womanly—the kind that won't look odd with a chiffon scarf or row of pearls. Choose trousers that suit your figure (this could mean narrow or a looser leg), but always keeping them as plain as possible. Recently, the trouser suit has been destructured. Stretch fabrics have revolutionised the way it fits and skims the body, visibly noticeable in the absence of darts and refined finish. Tread carefully with colour. A bright yellow or fuchsia pink suit will have a far shorter lifespan than the same outfit in a base shade. A trouser suit in a solid navy or neutral shade has the option of being lightened or darkened with what is worn underneath. Texture is important and is one of the ways in which designers have softened the trouser suit, adding a new dimension by tailoring in wool crepe, or one of the new silky weaves.

There are no specific criteria about how the classic trouser suit should look. Ultimately, the choice depends on body type. If you have a good posture, a softer slouch-shaped trouser suit will suit;

if you have long legs wider trousers work well; and you may need shoulder pads to compensate for narrow shoulders. What you wear with a trouser suit is important. A collar and tie, if not taken too seriously, can look incredibly feminine. Put pearls and tousled hair with pinstripes and a city suit turns sexy. Switch to cropped hair and the same outfit will become androgynous. Internationally, the trouser suit has been widely interpreted, and as a direct result of the trickle-down effect of fashion, most shapes can now be found at mass-market level. The Parisians, particularly Yves Saint Laurent and Dior, always adhere to a structured fit with shoulderline and waist defined. In Italy, Armani has single-handedly revolutionised the trouser suit; with his light touch, he created a jacket so fluid it can almost be called a blouse. The American approach is the most understated of all. Here the trouser suit is pared down to the absolute minimum, often without lapels and with concealed fastenings. The British trouser suit is the most difficult to define, but the most typical will probably have its roots in Savile Row—lots of ease and, depending on the designer, the odd element of quirkiness.

THE GREAT WHITE SHIRT

'The best kind are those that are literally a man's shirt for a woman. The shirt should have all the details: double cuffs, generous pleat set into the centre back, tails long enough to tuck in or knot on top. The collar has to look good standing up, or down. Good cloth is vital: two-fold cotton poplin, which has a slight sheen to it.'

MARTIN LEVITT, SHIRTMAKER, WEBSTER BROTHERS.

Above *The appeal of the great white skirt lies in its versatility, here, casual with collar upturned, sleeves rolled up and tails left out.*

We have always loved the solid, no nonsense great white shirt—the way it works with jeans or suits, and ingeniously illuminates the skin. Yet the fact is that it is almost impossible to find a woman's version of the great white shirt. All too often its understatement is undermined by unnecessary design detail and the great white shirt crosses the borderline into a blouse.

There is the natural temptation to take a short cut by borrowing or buying a man's—we have all tried that. But there are definite drawbacks. Apart from the dimensions (sleeve length and body width are often too large), the collar is the real telltale sign. Men's collars are cut to accommodate a muscular neck, and because of the depth of shirt stand and size often look odd on a woman. The ultimate great white shirt should have all the features of a man's but be proportionately smaller.

The type of cloth dictates how the shirt will look. Double fold cotton poplin is a very fine but densely woven cloth that wears well, keeps its structure and allows twin rows of tiny stitches without puckering. Pinpoint Oxford cotton has a slightly textured effect that softens on washing. These top quality cottons are often beyond the chain-store price range. At mass-market level, cloth varies so much that the only guideline is to look for medium, as opposed to featherweight cotton (try putting your hand behind the shirt—is it translucent?). At Webster Brothers and Pinks—two of the few traditional shirtmakers where off the peg shirts for women are made to Jermyn Street standards—a custom-made service is offered where shirts are constructed to meet your specification.

The white shirt on a woman has a great potential for versatility: you can play with the position of the collar—up or down, outside or in. Shirt tails go on show when the shirt doubles up as a jacket or tie into a knot at the front. Try leaving turnback cuffs open (provided the sleeves aren't too long) or fasten with clip-on earrings instead of cufflinks. The specific points to look for are plain, but even within a classic shirt, details vary considerably. The choice of collar is often made intuitively, but check whether it slots in with the rest of your wardrobe and that it suits your frame. Cuff depth is purely down to personal taste, but ideally it should correspond to the collar shape (a tiny collar and wide turnback cuff, for example, will look odd). On a practical level, the pleat at the centre back gives a more generous line.

Expert advice is one thing, but what do wearers look for? Model and actress Lauren Hutton, who virtually lives in white shirts, choses only those that are 'the best quality cotton, tight, tight weave with absolutely no frills or fashion, so it is ageless. A small unassertive collar, but the body big and roomy so you can do lots with it.' The hidden strength of the great white shirt is that it lends itself to improvisation. Watch the catwalks—designers have a talent for devising new ways of wearing it. Some suggestions: for day, frame the face by slightly raising the collar at the back making sure the front points downwards; wrap a long chiffon scarf under the collar, knotted in the same way as you would a tie; wear your strands of jewellery over or under the shirt. At night try leaving it open to the waist, tucking it securely (to prevent indecent exposure) into a full evening skirt. Mix it with other things—put a singlet or T-shirt underneath and knot the shirt on top. On the other hand, you could wear it in place of a jacket, but a word of warning: when the great white shirt takes on a starring role, make sure it's absolutely perfect.

GREAT WHITE SHIRT: KEY POINTS

- Try traditional men's shirtmakers—they often custom make for women.

- Good cloth is vital and can be detected instantly by its slight surface sheen.

- If you buy a man's shirt, always choose the smallest neck size.

- Know how you want to wear it. Make sure the collar looks good up or down, and the tails are long enough to be tied at the front.

- Bear in mind what you want to mix it with.

Left *Providing the fabric is substantial enough, a crisp white shirt can double as a jacket—left open, cuffs unbuttoned and worn with a singlet underneath.*

THE LITTLE BLACK DRESS

'I'm not someone who likes a lot of fuss—I always prefer to feel uncluttered. Black in itself demands to be plain—that's when it works best. But the main question is does it fit you? The black dress always looks perfect on its own, but it really depends on the face, the form. I have always loved the way dancers look—a neat head and beautiful face. The whole symmetry of a wonderful outline.'

JEAN MUIR, DESIGNER

'You always feel very comfortable in classic clothes. Perfectly all right, at ease. You can dress them up or down—by their very nature they provide a simple canvas for interesting and imaginative accessories.'

ANNA HARVEY,

DEPUTY EDITOR,

BRITISH *VOGUE*

The little black dress is every woman's answer to the last-minute invitation. Totally plain or dressed up with strong accessories, it eliminates time-wasting over colour-coding, and is unrivalled in its position as the wardrobe's passport to instant smartness.

On the High Street, rows of inexpensive little black dresses start appearing in stores around September in preparation for the party season. In almost every collection (provided you take a quick detour past the annual sequinned and appliqued numbers) there should be at least one basic little black dress which, with the right accessories, will be guaranteed to see you through several special occasions.

But note the cloth, detail, shade and cut. With something so pure, it's the subtleties that count. Before you buy, there is a specific sub-structure of important points to consider. First, take the colour. To the untrained eye, it's difficult to differentiate between shades of black—one looks much like another. But tonal variety can be found in the cloth, with velvet being the deepest and jersey probably the lightest. The key fabrics are velvet, wool crepe and jersey. Sometimes they are used in conjunction with each other as trimming or to define clever scissor-work. The actual choice will always be a question of personal preference, but note how it will act. Velvet, in silk or cotton, is by far the richest and most luxurious. Cotton velvet, because of its weight, works best in neat, slender proportions (remember it is warm and therefore more suited to winter). It is strong and if closely fitted, will streamline the body and behave like a corset. Silk velvet is more expensive, much lighter, with a higher shine and lends itself more easily to fluid shapes. Wool crepe is virtually uncreasable and has body. Satin backed crepe—textured on one side, slinky on the other—gives the option of matt or shine. For packing, jersey is unbeatable. Not only will it squeeze into the minutest space in the suitcase but more importantly can always be relied on to spring instantly back to life. On the body, jersey is

Right *Cut and cloth in perfect harmony in Jean Muir's little black dress.*

supple, will inevitably cling to every contour and should skim rather than hug. The most successful jersey dress shape is probably one that is fitted at the torso, extending into a flared, voluminous skirt at the bottom.

With something so pure, the cut is critical. A lot depends on your form, and preference for detail. Close up, the seamline's position is noticeable on a plain surface. But more importantly, remember: from a distance, the black dress creates a solid silhouette. Therefore, a good outline is critical, and utilised to the limit will accentuate the best parts of your anatomy: an elegant neck suits a shapely shoulderline, a well-toned back can be revealed with a cutaway, choose sleeveless if you have slender arms, or want to draw attention to a particularly decorative cuff.

The ultimate black dress is an understated base to work from. Therefore, as a general guideline, always choose plainness in preference to fuss. Avoid drapes, fiddly fastenings and, unless perfectly executed, complicated cutting. Proportion always relates to figure type, but the most versatile hem length (and one that won't break any dress codes) falls between mid-thigh and mid-calf. Adding a heel will elongate the silhouette.

Depending on how often you will wear it, the little black dress may be worth serious investment. At designer level, Jean Muir is internationally recognised as producing the most covetable and long-lasting. Her dresses are a combination of immaculate cutting—balancing the dress so that the cloth hangs perfectly—and exquisite design detail—a clever cuff, interesting fastening and seamlines expertly positioned at unusual angles. As a practical footnote, her signature fabrics jersey and wool crepe, both travel and wear well.

CLASSIC KNITS

'The prime considerations will always be comfort and versatility. In the classic market we are doing things that 30 years ago would have been impossible—particularly with very fine knits. There are many ways of identifying a good sweater, but the most reliable guide is the label.'

ANDREW MCROBB, MARKETING DIRECTOR, PRINGLE

The Lycra revolution eased us into a new way of thinking about clothes. As stretch bodies, leggings and wraps entered our wardrobes, the new dress code was having a curious effect on traditional knitwear. The classic staples—twinset, sweater and cardigan—were suddenly updated into contemporary proportions.

The star labels on the international knitwear circuit are: Pringle, McGeorge, Ballantyne, Glenmac, Barrie, Braemar, Hogg of Hawick, John Smedley, Lyle & Scott. Their expertise is sought by everyone who is anyone in fashion from Donna Karan to Chanel, safe in the knowledge that their quality is the best you can buy. Designers are aware that despite the advances in stretch textiles, knitwear is unique. In colour, versatility and feel, no weave, however inventive will ever come close. In the traditional mill-manufactured knit—and for a fraction of the designer price—you are paying for centuries of technical know-how: intarsias where each strand of yarn is transferred by hand (which means no bulk inside), fully fashioned shaping (eliminating chunky seams—all the curves are achieved by expert needlework), subtle reinforcements that guarantee a longer lifespan (knitted tape sewn into stress points) and yarns that are only second to cashmere—Geelong lambswool and merino wool.

The quality of chain-store knitwear varies enormously. At Marks & Spencer, who pride themselves on producing excellent lower-priced knitwear, the best buys are anything in ribbed cotton, Aran, Fair Isle and basic classic lambswool cardigans and crew necked sweaters. Generally, the fail-safe guide to finding a great knit is to know your yarns. The label inside tells you the exact fibre content: choose pure wool if possible, but at a pinch, settle for a high proportion of it blended with a small amount of synthetic yarn. Cotton is naturally popular for summer because it has an in-built ability to breathe. Superwash wool has an elasticity that makes it survive rigorous spins in a washing machine. Remember, synthetics, particularly acrylic, do not have the same ability to tune into your body temperature and tend to retain static when washed. Synthetics work best in tight ribs—voluminous garments, like tunics, are prone to misshaping.

You now know what to look for, but what about fit? Stretch equals easy sizing, but there are still key areas to watch. The neckline, in any shape or form should pull easily over the head. Polo necks are often too long and end up curving under the chin—try a turtle neck (which gives a similar effect) instead. V-necks are tricky if you want to wear them without anything underneath—always make sure the depth is correct. The type of stitchwork (whether it is totally ribbed or a combination of different tensions) determines where and how it fits on the body—this is relevant to the pieces you will want to pair it with (for example, whether the sweater is to be worn inside or out). Length is another key area: check whether it peeps below your jacket and always keep slightly shorter if you want to put a cardigan on top.

'Classic means quality.'

INÈS DE LA FRESSANGE, FASHION DESIGNER AND FORMER CHANEL HOUSE MODEL

Above *A new angle on the polo-neck sweater achieved by varying stitchwork – wider on the body, finer at the neck.*

The last word belongs to the most desirable yarn of all—cashmere. Because of its rarity it is not only wonderfully luxurious, but extremely expensive. Even though price-points fall occasionally, the notion of owning a genuine cashmere remains, for most of us, far beyond our wildest dreams. But help is at hand. Try the sales (sometimes you can find that elusive cashmere if you are first in the queue). Alternatively, visit border mill factory shops where they often sell slightly damaged cashmeres at affordable prices. Before you buy, remember longevity is not necessarily proportionate to price. Treat your cashmere with care. Washed gently (by hand and dried flat), repaired immediately if there are any snags, and rested regularly to allow the fibres to regain their structure, and a cashmere sweater can last a lifetime. At three score years and ten, a sound investment.

MODERN CLASSICS

'They allow your personality to come through and because they are basics in the true sense of the word, offer an anonymous base for dressing up. I choose thick cotton jersey T-shirts from men's departments and often buy jeans second hand because they look far better worn in. Modern classics are great plain, but also accessorised with clean abstract or an antique piece of jewellery.'

HELEN STOREY, DESIGNER

Modern classics are the kind of clothes super models pull on after a day spent posing in haute couture. They are the casual trio that survived the Fifties work-wear revolution—the eternal T-shirt, denim jeans and the leather biker jacket.

Top of the list is the T-shirt: a great summer stand-by that isn't only for holidays, but can be slipped under a tailored jacket or dressed up with jewellery. Longer versions masquerade as dresses; knotted at the side, they double-up as alternative nightwear in winter. The basic T-shirt—scoop neck, half sleeves, loose fit—is probably the cheapest item (bar a singlet) that you can buy and is found all year round in any chain store. How do you select the best? T-shirts are often ready-wrapped, so, like a man's white shirt, your view is obliterated by glossy packaging. First rule: don't take the size at face value—assess the measurement by looking at T-shirts on show. Never be deluded into thinking bigger looks better (outsized proportions equals half-sleeves that end up past your elbow); choose one that is roomy but not so bulky that it won't tuck into trousers. Analyse it: a nicely proportioned neck (not too tight or too wide) with an elas-

CLASSIC KNITS: KEY POINTS

● Know how to care for your knitwear—wash according to the instructions, repair holes or stray yarns immediately.

● The cuffs and hem are always the first part of a sweater to fray—make sure these are stitched securely at the seam.

● Cardigans should look good inside and out. Remember they are often worn open—as the interior is on view, it must be well finished.

● Try men's wear departments for knitted waistcoats and oversized fishermen's sweaters.

● Always look at the label for percentages of pure wool or cotton content.

Left *Contemporary thinking puts a new twist on the traditional twinset. Note the longer length, generous fit and higher tie neck.*

Far right *Putting a new perspective on the biker jacket with the addition of chunky jewellery and a tulle dancing dress.*

Right *The T-shirt and Denim jeans are staples of the modern classic dress code.*

Above *Looks familiar: the biker jacket grows into a coat, but keeps the key details of zip, black leather and asymmetrical fastening.*

ticated ribbed edge, securely hemmed to stop stretch and good quality jersey (soft and slightly thick to touch), which allows bounce-back after washing, are musts.

American work wear left fashion with a great legacy—denim jeans. A no-age classic, denim is solid, dependable, with a cast-iron reputation for durability. In common with the British-made mac, denims are the only other classic that actually improves with age. For decades jeans were pigeonholed exclusively as casual wear, but designer dress codes have changed all that—denim even hit haute couture when Chanel sliced it with tweed in their signature suits. Toughness has always been denim's greatest asset—the trademark rivets and double stitching a unique way to reinforce stress points. For the purists, nothing can surpass the tradition of soaking in the bath and letting them shrink to your shape. In time, denim will lighten gradually from indigo to pale blue, but if you don't want to wait, speed up the process by buying ready-faded. Although the price range in the jean market is incredibly wide, there is actually very little difference—except in fit and label status - between designer denims and traditional Levi or Wrangler jeans. Denims have a surprising new blueprint: indigo is no longer *de rigueur* and jeans can be brilliants, pastel, white and print—anything from candy stripe to mega polka dots. The other great change is the way denim can now mix toughness with stretch. Jeans are the only classic that

Below *One of Ralph Lauren's recurring themes taken literally. Military style plays a major part in all of his collections.*

Above *The unmistakable Chanel suit, probably the most plagiarised, by far the most famous of all designer classics, and still top of the most-wanted list 40 years after its creation.*

Right *A sporty take on the Chanel suit achieved with the addition of singlet and ankle socks, but keeping the signature signs of camellia, chain belt and rows of pearls.*

are acceptably distressed. But be careful how you wear them. Strategically ripped or frayed jeans (so long as they are a tight fit) look great paired with a crisp white shirt and plimsolls. Brand new, try buying a few sizes too big, pulled in with a Western belt.

The black leather jacket says rock 'n' roll, motorbikes, and is the only classic with a rebellious streak. It has the basic criteria for dressing in double-quick time: no-need-to-match-black, indestructible material (nothing lasts longer than leather), a loop-through bucklet belt and the greatest fastening of the twentieth century, the zip, angled asymmetrically at the front (so you never snag your T-shirt in the rush), and vertically at the cuffs for high speed. Where to buy one? Remember, it takes time, effort and a lot of wear and tear for new leather to achieve that lived-in look. Take a whiz around second-hand stores that specialise in trade-ins. Avoid logos and coloured leathers, which have a limited novelty value. The black leather jacket can be whatever you want it to be: ride the freeway in leather jeans and biker boots. Take that same leather jacket and put it with unlikely partners—a singlet and tulle skirt for eveningwear with a streetwise attitude.

DESIGNER CLASSICS

'Karl Lagerfeld has taught us the way to wear classics is to undermine their seriousness. You can have it both ways—you can have a beautiful serious garment twinned with jeans or leather, always with the accessory of the moment.'

SARAH MOWER, FASHION JOURNALIST

The designer classic is the brilliant idea that eclipses thousands of throwaway ones. For Azzedine Alaïa it was the discovery of body consciousness; Donna Karan's claim to fame was putting stretch in the work place; Armani reworked the trouser suit.

Designer classics should never be confused with the inspired seasonal design. Take the Chanel suit. Since Coco invented it, it is probably the most plagiarised designer classic of all time. The real McCoy is made from tweed, has double 'C' buttons, signature lining and a hidden secret—a tiny chain discreetly stitched inside at the point where the lining and hemline meet. Even Vivienne Westwood, the English innovator who is notoriously quirky and quick off the mark, has her own off-the-wall classics. Her breast-skimming corset, first seen in the mid-Eighties, was based on an 18th-century original, and has since been a permanent fixture in her collection. Westwood explains: 'I took an old pattern, made it in modern fabric, elasticated side panels and

'Classics are real clothes, never costume. Pieces you want to keep putting on— the kind of things you never tire of.'

PEGGY PASCHAYAN, COORDINATOR, DONNA KARAN'S DKNY RANGE

MODERN CLASSICS: KEY POINTS

- Break the rules: mix jeans with tailored jacket, singlet with a dancing skirt, put a biker jacket with a ballgown.

- Stick to top chain stores for T-shirts.

- Distressed denim works best with smarter elements (e.g. good tailoring, chic jewellery).

- Always buy a plain biker jacket—you can customise it later.

- Don't forget the alternative modern classics—denim jacket, chinos, chambray shirt.

DESIGNER CLASSICS: KEY POINTS

• Add your own trimming to basic outfits—that could mean braid, gilt buttons or sailor stripes.

• Designer classics are often inspired by traditional outfitters.

• Analyse the prediction pages—spot the recurring styles, particularly if you feel an affinity with one designer.

• Take into account the way clothes are accessorised.

• Cheap versions of tried-and-tested designer classics can always be found in chain stores—the trick is recognising which has hidden potential.

transformed it into something that could be sold off the peg in a shop.' Over the years, she has reworked it using print, denim and draping.

It could be that the designer classic is not down to one particular piece, but is more a recognisable look. Ralph Lauren, whose style is mostly rooted in the great outdoors, has the rare talent of taking the simplest clothes synonymous with everyday American life—a riding mac, Navaho blanket, corduroy jodhpurs—and making them desirable by expertly updating and styling.

How do designer-priced classics fit in with the philosophy of *More Dash Than Cash?* As a starting point they are invaluable. The secret of achieving designer looks on a budget is to improvise. The only way to do *that* is by picking out the recurring pieces in the prediction pages. Take that know-how and add your imagination. It could be down to the way a look is achieved. A basic chain-store tweed suit becomes a copycat Chanel if piled high with pearls and gilt chains. Your version of an Yves Saint Laurent tuxedo (whose popularity put a new perspective on women's evening wear) could, if you were discerning enough, be a curvy antique one with a satin collar. A Lacroix lookalike, on the other hand, may be an irreverent mix of colour and texture. Emulate Ralph Lauren by scouting around *his* sources of inspiration—military, equestrian outfitters and Santa Fe stores.

But what if only the real thing will do? One option is to sift carefully through the sale rail at designer stores, where classics are sometimes slashed to half price. Or scour second-hand stores—particularly those situated in up-market areas. The odds on finding a Chanel suit in the right size and colour might be a million to one, but it just might be your lucky day.

CLASSIC ACCESSORIES

'Accessories have always been the unsung heroes of fashion, yet they are the key pieces that will make or break an outfit. A good belt has the ability to totally transform a simple dress, bags must be aesthetically pleasing as well as practical. Like clothes, accessories are about getting proportions right and should be chosen in the same way—assess whether the belt is the correct width and length; bags must always relate to your height and build.'

JOHN AND MONIQUE DAVIDSON,
ACCESSORY DESIGNERS, LONDON

Classic accessories, like classic clothes, are those that have survived the whims of fashion. They are the vital ingredients of the

Vivienne Westwood's corsets where key changes are colour and fabric, but the structure remains the same.
Above *Elegantly draped.*
Top left *Salon-printed denim.*
Top right *Boucher print.*
Left *Delicate silk twill.*

Above *Accessories can add a plain or ornamental edge to classic dressing.*

international collections and, ironically, often say more than the clothes. The simple decision between putting an elegant leather loafer in place of a sturdy lace-up shoe could be as crucial as the designer colour story or silhouette. The classic accessory is anything from a plimsoll to a string of pearls. It is not necessarily luxurious, or expensive, and never outrageous. Across the board, the common denominator of any classic is comfort, minimum detailing and simple styling.

Classic shoes never contort the foot; they are flattering, are slipped on, or laced up—and then forgotten about. There are no dressy details—bows, shoestring straps criss-crossing up the leg. The basic classic shoe trio is the brogue, loafer and plimsoll. The loafer, a low-heeled slip-on shoe, is a close relation to the moccasin. Often, in leather, the texture is so tough and shoe cut so low that it tends to cause gaping at the side when walking. The suede loafer—Gucci's snaffle front shoe, by far the most imitated—is usually more practical as it is a more snug fit and is generally cut higher up the foot. Brogues, a low-heeled lace up, which can be plain or patterned with punch holes, sometimes look too macho on a woman. The loafer works with a skirt and trousers, but tread carefully with the brogue and watch how you wear it. When buying, the actual quality of the leather is probably the most important consideration, and note the proportion—not too clumpy or thick soled. Plimsolls, originally designed with treads to stop slipping on board ship, are found in navy or white and are undoubtedly the cheapest form of summer footwear (they look great without laces—try this only if cut high enough on the foot). There are alternatives: the ballet pump (must be beautifully done—like the little black dress, its plainness means no concession for less than perfect proportions), the jodhpur boot (usually tan or black—look for those with strong elastic), the court shoe (classic ones have nicely shaped heels—not too spiky or chunky), the co-respondent shoe (in cream or navy and white, flat or with a heel—make sure you have the right clothes to wear with it). Check for classic points of quality: leather soles, although visually attractive (especially when you cross your legs and the soles are on show) are not necessarily the most hard wearing, but look for leather inside to help the foot breathe.

Another key accessory is the belt, which does far more than define the waistline. The belt's main function is to hold clothes in place—pulled through trousers it will position the garment and at the same time prevent your shirt or sweater from sliding out. A good quality belt will be in bridle leather, completely lined and possibly hand stitched. The buckle is the centrepoint—look for solid brass or solid silver. Always buy one size up from your waist measurement to accommodate extra fabric. When trying on, the buckle should comfortably slot through the second hole in the belt to allow for possible expansion.

The classic bag can be anything from a satchel to a leather rucksack, but the most famous are the Kelly and the quilted Chanel bag (always with its signature chain). The size and style of bag is entirely dependent on your needs—whether you carry a lot or not. Look for richness in everything—leather (even if it is only used as trimming), handles must be attached with rivets or brass D-rings; zips should be solid, and of good quality as they form the most-used part of the bag.

Jewellery, real or fake, is a classic if it is plain. The pearl in any form (string, choker, stud earrings) is an always stylish accessory. Chains look best in gold; silver lends itself to pure lines.

ACCESSORIES: KEY POINTS

- Repair shoes before they are beyond repair.

- Bags should be beautiful but at the same time fit in with your lifestyle.

- Note the width of the belt— will it slot through your trouser loops?

- Your accessories must tie in together, although not necessarily match.

- Give your accessories proper attention—treat leather with leather food, and brush up suede.

'I don't believe in the word. If you call it classic it's because women want it and want it.'

MANOLO BLAHNIK,

SHOE DESIGNER

GROOMING

Wonderful clothes are the starting blocks of good style, but at some point they pass the baton to you. How many marks out of ten would you give your physical appearance, the feet and inches that stand in front of the mirror? Be honest: no one's going to know. Does your skin look clear, are you pleased with your posture, are you well-groomed or, frankly, unkempt? Women who protest that time spent on grooming has no place in their busy diaries forget that a controlled, well-maintained appearance may say much about their self-respect and their ability to cope. Grooming is not an indulgence: little and often is a more rewarding philosophy than spasmodic lengthy repair work, and getting up ten minutes earlier to file your nails or do something interesting with your hair poses no threat to the most frenetic of lifestyles.

Left *Relaxed, confident, in control . . . she is complete.*

Grooming is about self-discipline, about setting yourself realistic targets and restructuring your life to make time for a good night's sleep, for a regular haircut, for a skincare regime. Concentrating on one area is not enough; the secret is to look good all over. That means starting with an inner contentment, a fresh complexion, glossy hair and well-kept hands and feet—everything in peak condition—and finishing with the styles and colours that make appearance versatile. Good grooming varies your looks subtly without making you a spectacle. It's not a question of immaculate but untouchable women who spend hours in beauty salons; it can be looser and fresh, but it has to be deliberate. Interestingly, when asked who she would label as well-groomed, top British designer Jean Muir listed Annie Lennox, Madonna and Lauren Bacall, who are very individual in their methods, but all three consciously *create* their look.

Grooming has little to do with beauty. No woman should feel despondent if she's not truly beautiful. Beauty is something nature intended and a matter of chance and genes; it depends on who's looking and what's fashionable—and fortunate and rare is someone born with exactly the right characteristics at just the right time. Feeling beautiful—the *joie de vivre*, the twinkle in the eye so much admired—is altogether different, and comes from confidence, which stems from looking one's best. Grooming is something we can work on, something with which we can experiment, express our identity and moods and add another dimension to our clothes. Even a beauty has to be well-groomed. It may require you to keep abreast of fashions in make-up, changes in proportions between clothes and volume of hair; no one's suggesting you alter your lifestyle dramatically. Obsessive behaviour is not the issue here; in its place, a regular, moderate regime that maximises what you have naturally, so that you can say with confidence, as Iman, one of the world's most beautiful models, once quipped, 'Some bits of me could be better, but the overall package is great.'

ORGANISATION . . .

. . . is key. You have to be able to see all your make-up, brushes, hair ties and grips at a glance to inspire something a little different quickly each morning. No one has sufficient time before work to scrabble about trying to find a particular lipstick. Try to keep everything together, not some in the bathroom, and bits dotted all over your bedroom. Arrange your make-up, hair and skincare products in rows in a box in a drawer, or on a plain metal

Left Clothes and grooming are the orchestration, but you have to be able to see the conductor.

tray on a table top. Baskets for make-up look pretty, but inside, everything's jumbled, so chips and soon looks dirty; clean, well-kept make-up is more likely to sustain your interest to the end of the bottle. Lay out brushes next to your hair dryer, and prop up hair pins and pencils in small empty jars. Everything should be next to a mirror, its back and your face to the light. Sitting may be steadier for applying make-up, but standing up repeatedly to face a full-length mirror lets you check everything works with your clothes. Pin up a rota of all the grooming jobs you need to do—pedicure, manicure, washing brushes, etc.—and work through it, ten minutes on one each evening. And if one day a hairstyle or particular make-up really works with specific clothes, make a note for next time.

SKIN

Nothing deadens a wonderful jacket or shirt like a dull and life-less complexion. Skin needs a healthy glow, and a smooth, un-blemished face is the only canvas for make-up. Few people's skin is so perfect that they can ignore it altogether and the results of harsh treatment quickly show. Extreme cold, biting winds, excessive sun, drying central heating, air conditioning and too much alcohol all have a negative effect. Rosy cheeks examined closely may in fact be broken veins.

Stress, diet, hormone imbalance, exercise, sleep, smoke and sun all affect the condition of skin. The first three are often the bug bears behind spots, and too little sleep results in grey, puffy, poor-textured skin. Make sure you drink enough water to flush away toxins—up to a litre a day if you can—and, since elimination of waste is vital, stick to a diet with a high fibre content. That means eating plenty of fruit, vegetables, wholemeal grains, bran, beans, etc., supplementing them with good quality protein and watching your intake of fat, salt, white sugar, coffee and tea, and junk foods like crisps and sweets, which for spots are like holding a red rag to a bull. Cooking methods also affect the skin's appearance, as well as the nutritional value of foods—grilling and steaming are healthier than frying. The full extent of the ravages inflicted by smoke on the skin is only just coming to light. Most

FACE FACTS

How much you spend on skin care products depends on your budget and how special they make you feel. Though problem areas qualify for attention, remember the beauty industry has its own interests at heart as well as yours, and be cautious about being dragged way out of your budget by glossy advertising campaigns.

• **Don't** pay extra for smart packaging and a glamorous name. If you really object to the look of some cheaper makes, decant the contents into the simple plastic bottles you can buy in most chemists.

• **Do** ask for samples of products—some companies offer free in-store facials— to check they don't irritate your skin before investing big sums.

• **Do** check babycare products—they're generally unscented, cheaper and milder.

• **Do** wait for new technology to trickle down from premium ranges to middle-market products. Think how quickly sunscreens were incorporated into some of the cheaper moisturisers.

• **Don't** fall for new marketing buzz-words, which are often meaningless and just pump up the price. Skin care consultant Eve Lom explains: "Hypo-allergenic" doesn't guarantee *you* won't have a reaction; nothing except distilled water is non-allergenic to everyone. "Nourishing" is misleading too—foods added may smell delicious but very little can "feed" the skin unless you eat it.'

• **Do** keep things simple. Some skin specialists argue that the added ingredients about which expensive ranges boast could cause an adverse reaction from some skins.

people can recognise the yellowish, lined look so characteristic of cigarette smokers who deprive their skin of some of the oxygen it needs, but recent research now suggests that all smoke—cigarette, industrial or exhaust—has a negative effect *on* the skin. Basically, smoke contains free radicals, which are molecules that have lost an electron. They speed up the breakdown of the skin by trying to steal electrons back from the skin's own molecules: the net result is premature ageing. But it's not all doom and gloom. The good news is that vitamins E and C—preferably both since vitamin E is more potent when in conjunction with vitamin C—help counter smoke's devastation. While many doctors are encouraging us to consume more of these vitamins, the skin can be treated directly: several creams contain vitamin E, but Estée Lauder and Clarins have both created formulations that also encapsulate the less stable vitamin C.

Unfortunately, using twice as many beauty products doesn't make you doubly beautiful. In fact, putting too much on your skin could prompt a sensitivity, clog up pores and inhibit the skin's natural protection. Skin is a barrier stopping moisture getting out and pollutants in, so don't over pull or scrub it; break it and you're quickly into the realms of sensitivities and allergies. The ground rule is to keep things simple. 'All those creams for specific areas like eyes and necks are so unnecessary. What next? A toe cream?' says Eve Lom pointedly.

Proper cleansing goes a long way to achieving a healthy balanced complexion. Choose a cleanser appropriate to your skin type—either a lotion, cream, cleansing bar, soap or facial wash. It will slough off make-up, stale perspiration salts, oil and dead cells from the skin's surface. A normal skin with no make-up may need no other cleanser than soap and water twice a day, but dry skins can find soap over-harsh and react better to cream cleansers, even more than lotions; oilier skins prefer lighter lotions and cleansing bars that leave them feeling grease-free. Exfoliation will go one step further, but avoid violent rubbing so you expose a clean bloom and not sore, dry patches.

Some skin care specialists recommend you use a toner, which does remove all traces of a cleanser, close the pores and produce a cool, refreshing feeling, but realistically can be skipped altogether. Any containing alcohol should definitely be avoided if the skin is dry, and you can make your own milder, cheap versions from a weak solution of witch hazel in rose water, or a basin of warm water softened with a spoonful of bicarbonate of soda.

Moisturisers, on the other hand, are critical, not so much because they add water but because they prevent water loss. Dry

Below *A fresh complexion often speaks for itself and doesn't need much prompting from make-up.*

Above *Black skin contains large amounts of melanin, the skin's natural defence against sun damage, but fair skins are not equipped to deal with strong sunlight and like it or not should keep out of the sun forever more. Much of the damage we attribute to ageing – wrinkling, sagging, sallow colouring, visible blood vessels and brown spots – is in fact due to sun exposure. Research shows that whilst many high SPF products provide protection against the UVB waves responsible for burning the upper layers of the skin, many offer only minimal or no protection against the UVA waves that reach deep down into the skin's dermis and destroy its structure. The motto being: choose your sunscreen wisely.*

skins tend to be rough and broken so water easily escapes; the moisturiser effectively acts like a sealant, but shouldn't be greasy enough to plug pores. If your skin's oily, some specialists would argue you don't need one at all, except a little round the eyes. Some moisturisers will double as cleansers, and many models use them to wipe away make-up because they're so gentle. Cheap aqueous creams bought over the chemist's counter have merit because they contain no perfume or colouring, but try to use them only at night because they won't contain the single most important ingredient for daylight—that is, a sunscreen.

Shades of the future

Until recently, it was thought skin looked better with a tan. It's true sun can warm up the chill of icy, white skin, but in good condition, clean, fresh skin with a good circulation, however pale, can be incredibly beautiful. The damage inflicted by the sun's UV rays outweighs the benefits by far. Apart from the very real risk of developing skin cancer, especially by fair skins, uneven pigmentation and 80 per cent of the visible signs of ageing are now attributed to overexposure to sun. Whilst UVB rays burn, UVA penetrates to the lower levels of the skin, and damages the collagen and elastin, so that the skin loses its firmness. Rather like a soft plum, skin left in the sun will dry, become harder and crinkle into a wizened prune; Buddhist monks who deny themselves daylight during their life are largely wrinkle-free even when old.

There are two schools of thought concerning sunscreens at the moment: the purists who won't let the sun reach their skin at all, who use UV filters even in ordinary daylight, and those who protect themselves only in harsh sunlight. In strong sun you should wear a sunscreen of SPF 15 or more, with filters that absorb both UVA and B rays. If you're skiing, use a sunscreen that's specifically designed for even higher sun intensity, won't freeze on the face and is waterproof. For everyday wear? Even the cheaper moisturisers contain a sunscreen now, and they're certainly more reasonably priced than some of the so-called anti-ageing creams.

Say aaah . . .

Keeping the skin well-circulated with blood encourages a healthy bloom. Squinting, grinning and grimacing every morning for two minutes will rev the circulation—which takes toxins away—as well as isolate neglected muscles and prevent them sagging. Diana Vreeland, editor of American *Vogue* in the Sixties, reasoned that French women don't have slack faces because they exercise their jaws and sides of the face just getting their words out: 'Say *"Che-rie"!'* she said. 'Did you see what your face just did, all the exercise you got? Now try "Dear".' She had a point.

Body work

The sight of a bare shoulder or a silky leg framed by a fine fabric can be sensual or an utter eyesore. No one without a year-round caring strategem can expect to emerge from a winter's quota of cocooning sweaters and cover-up trousers with smooth, glossy bareness. A skin-softening soak in the bath is the best place to start. Ideally, the water should be at body temperature, which is 37°C; any higher and it'll dry out your skin and encourage broken capillaries. Staying in too long is equally drying, so after you've been in for a minute or so, try rubbing your skin with your finger, and if little rolls of dead skin appear, you need a body scrub. Dead skin left on the surface has a lacklustre look, and when hairs can't push through this dead layer, unsightly hard pimples form. With a loofah, or a handful of sea salt between you and a towelling mit, gently rub your body with circular movements to expose a healthy bloom. Rinse it all away, and then massage in copious amounts of body lotion so the skin looks firmer. Further plus points of a regular body rub are that it invigorates a sluggish

MARIE HELVIN'S SKIN TIPS

Since the seventies, Marie Helvin has modelled for most top magazines. Her advice for keeping skin in peak condition is engagingly budget-based and simple.

• 'Here are 3 cheap ways of creating skin-softening baths. For one, I cut the heel from a stocking, fill it with oatmeal, tie it and throw it in the bath. The water becomes milky and rich.

• Secondly, I save all the peel from the satsumas I eat. At bathtime I throw a handful into the water. The tangerine oil leaves a thin film on my skin.

• When perfume counters bombard me with samples, I take them all. I keep a container of cooking oil by the bath and empty a couple of samples into it. It makes a luxurious, cheap bath oil.

• To create an excellent skin cream, I spend an afternoon breaking capsules of vitamin E and synthetic vitamin A into a cheap face cream like Ponds. It has to be synthetic because natural vitamin A is usually in fish oil form and can contain carotin; and you don't want to smell or go orange!

• In winter, when my skin is dry, I put margarine on my face before using soap; it makes the soap less drying.'

• I throw very little out of the kitchen. I use a lot of fruit and vegetables on my face. Puréed avocado, for example, feels great on the skin.

blood supply to the skin and may stimulate the lymphatic drainage systems that keep cellulite at bay. Bath oils and preparations that soften the water will help to keep the skin supple, but some bubble baths are too harsh and can cause irritation. Grooming is about paying attention to details such as elbows and knees, for which sunflower or almond oils are efficient softeners, especially when mixed with a little salt to lift off dead flakes.

Keep up to date with removing leg hair: shiny stubble poking through stockings is off-putting to say the least, and bare legs should always be smooth. Waxing 'zips' hair out from the root, so lasts longer than other methods—generally from two to three weeks, but it's a technique that requires practice. Instructions for chemical depilatories need careful reading in order to minimise irritation, and you should always do a patch test before covering the whole leg. Shaving is the fastest, most economical method. For best results, keep the leg clear of oils and creams that could block a clean razor, wet and soap well, and shave against the direction of growth, which varies over the leg.

Left *Back to front: even less accessible zones need consistent attention.*

THE FINER POINTS

Lips must be smooth to work as a base for lipstick. If touching them feels like prodding dry empty craters, lipstick will only collect and look dirty. Try a tip from the models backstage at the shows: rub in lip salve or Vaseline until the lips become soft; then use a toothbrush to gently ease off dead skin flakes. Apply lip salve regularly, one preferably that contains a sunscreen.

Eyes need sleep and a healthy diet to look their best. Too much alcohol and reading in bad light will also affect their sparkle and may encourage red thread veins. Dark circles under the eyes are more likely to be a family trait than a consequence of lack of sleep or disease, but puffiness usually means there's been too much cream left round the eyes. If you do put a moisturiser in the eye area, blot it gently after a minute or two. And avoid pearly eye shadows that draw attention to the problem. An old pick-me-up for eyes still has worth: massage the back of your neck and lie down for ten minutes with your feet slightly raised and cold compresses—cucumber slices or a cold flannel—over the lids.

Above *Regular foot care keeps feet looking great, but can also improve posture, prevent annoyances such as tights snagging and, since many nerves terminate in the feet, could even instill a sense of well-being.*

Teeth need frequent, thorough brushing, flossing and regular trips to the dentist—at least every six months. It's also worth seeing the hygienist once a year who'll scrape off any unsightly tartar that collects just above the gums. Be vigilant about brushing, at

least twice a day, including the tongue: apart from being corrosive, plaque is also foul smelling. A toothbrush shouldn't last longer than three months and for a mid-term boost, dip it into an antiseptic mouthwash. Jerry Hall's reputed method for whitening her teeth—rubbing a lemon over them and smiling at the sun—mustn't be attempted without cleaning your teeth afterwards to remove the acid!

Eyebrow shape is frequently at the mercy of fashion, so it's important never to do anything drastic. Plucking away a few straggling hairs is fine, provided you only work from below. Other than with make-up you won't be able to improve on the shape nature gave you, so leave the top layer well alone. In general, the outer end of the brow shouldn't extend beyond an imaginary line from the edge of the nose to the outer corner of the eye and up. To make plucking less excruciating, wash your face with warm water so the skin is soft, but never pluck just before going somewhere special: one factor of good grooming is to make it look effortless—it's no big secret if you appear with red blotches. If reddening does occur, lay on a bag of ice.

Hands and feet are details that count as much as other parts of your appearance. Constant care is more beneficial than an occasional manicure. 'Nails are the *sine qua non* of good grooming,' Polly Sellar, British *Vogue*'s Beauty Editor, once declared. 'Nothing is more attractive than neat, shortish, white-tipped nails that are prettily shaped and just a hint glossier and pinker than nature.' There's no need to grow your nails long - too often they break unevenly and look dirty. Better to put a few minutes aside once a week to file them, in one direction only, flat across the top, with straight sides and only slightly curved edges. If one does snap, quickly file the others short. Almond oil massaged into and under the nails once a day will keep them flexible so they break less often and the cuticles are soft enough to be teased back. In particular, deep red polish should be retouched the minute a chip appears because 'a single chink in a glamorous veneer is enough to ruin the whole appearance', warned *Vogue*. The hands themselves often age faster than other parts of the body, so keep a tube of rich hand cream by the sink and wear rubber gloves for cleaning. Vaseline rubbed in and tissued off will generally remove any ingrained dirt.

Even when your feet won't be on display, use a pumice stone to slough away hard skin. Then slather on heavy cream and buff or put polish on the nails. A foot bath—warm water sprinkled

with a handful of Epsom salts—will soften the skin and be wonderfully stimulating for the rest of the body too. But if your feet
emerge from winter in a too-wicked condition, it's worthwhile investing in a pedicure or a chiropody treatment to start the ball
rolling. If you constantly have hard skin in certain areas, you
might think about reassessing the way you walk, or at least how
well your shoes fit. In general, bright red toenails look good with
most skin tones, and most colours of clothes.

Far left *Grooming is a timeless commodity: Grace Kelly, photographed in the Fifties, could be primed for the Nineties too.*

HAIR

Long hair is wonderful provided it's well cut, glossy and you feel
happy with it; on the other hand, cutting it can be the lift you
need. A short sexy crop with an infectious boyishness has infinite
appeal. If you can't keep long hair smooth or lusciously wild, forget it altogether. Limp long hair is horrible.

When choosing a style it's important to think about the way
you live. A cut that needs lengthy blow-drying or long hair held
up with pins and spray may look wonderful in a magazine, but
have you the time and patience to keep it that way? The best
styles are effortlessly versatile. Short, softly graduated hair, or a

Left *A few shakes and it's dry.*

Above *All it takes is effort and a little imagination: supermodel Karen Mulder in remarkably different guises.*

swing cut that follows your own hair patterns and needs little care are lifesavers if you're constantly racing the clock, yet don't preclude variables if the pressure suddenly turns off. For example, they can be slicked back with modelling gel, blow-dried smooth over a rounded brush, scrunch-dried to a tousled effect, or rollered on the top layers for extra bounce and volume.

Fashions in hair ricochet between long and short, but look before you leap from one to the other: hair only grows about six inches a year, and even if fashion does have a wave of short back and sides, give yourself time to work the urge into or out of your system first. Take on board your personality. When your character is swamped by a look, the look dies too. Think how ridiculous TV presenter Paula Yates's flamboyant bleached hair spun up into a beehive would seem on, say, the serene Jane Seymour. Your hair should complement the way you talk and walk, whether you're effervescent or placid etc. Also think of the type of people you have to meet; don't treat the boss to a sudden change—he or she might not understand your fashion statements.

Most of all, take heed of your clothes. Voluminous, bouncing curls may look superb with a soft, lean silhouette—a tailored trouser suit, as on the cover of this book for example—but worn with sugar-sweet colours and fussy shapes, they're the trademarks of a dizzy bimbo. A sleek head can look lost above a huge, bear-like coat, but when worn with something long and lean is impressively understated. Think, too, about collars. How will shoulder-length hair sit on a big shawl-collar? Will it be bent in directions it shouldn't go? Should you wear long hair inside or outside a coat? And when you wear that perfect white shirt will anyone be able to see whether the collar's turned up or down? The shape and height of a hat, especially, must complement your hair. As a general guideline, push your hair well back or you'll be swamped. Bear in mind, too, how your hair will emerge once you take the hat off.

Hair needs considered attention to look its best. Everyone can tell the difference between carefree tresses and a matted bird's nest. We have, more than any generation, all manner of styling products and equipment at our disposal, so shame on you if you grumble that you can't be bothered. Model Karen Mulder is a lesson in variety, who in each runway show can coax something different from her long blonde locks: loosely waved with no make-up she plays up her freshness; backcombed into a peak-volume mane she's more glamorous and sexy, and looped up into big pincurls she turns into a modern-day vamp. What's clear in each look is how critical the follow-through with the right make-up is. For instance, don't kill healthy bubbly curls with pancake-thick foundation; or use just a cautious smidgen of brown eyeliner if you have hair like a silver-screen goddess.

Hairdressers: how to get the right result
When you pay so much money, it's perfectly reasonable to check out a stylist before booking an appointment. Personal recommendation can't be bettered, but otherwise ask for a free consultation—and if it's not free, walk out. The telltale signs to look for are whether the towels and gowns are fresh, whether the surfaces are clear of debris and sneaking a look at the staff helps too. If you're still worried, book in for a blow-dry. You can judge a hairdresser by the way the hair is handled. Pay the most you can afford—when you spend so much on clothes you use only now and again, you should budget for hair you wear every day—and clarify whether coffee, conditioners, etc. are extra.

Many women are made timid by hairstylists—there's something about being seen at your worst, coupled with the fact you can't always see what they're doing. It's important to talk through your style before your hair's wet. But how do you get your message across? 'It's best to be open-minded,' advises Nicky Clarke, one of London's top stylists. 'The client doesn't want to be dictated to and nor does the stylist. They both want to create something good, so there shouldn't be a fight. Brief words on your way of life are useful but to reach the levels of style she aspires to, the client should really take advice.' Try to stay with the same stylist and give him a second chance if you're less than happy to begin with: so often he won't be able to tell how your hair behaves until he's dried it for the first time.

Sometimes a quick trim may be all a style needs to remove split ends and put back bounce. A straight blunt edge, so attractive in a bob, must never be allowed to get wispy. Shorter styles should be recut every three to four weeks, long hair more like every eight. Keep on top of appointments. 'There are only vague rules about which styles best suit,' says Nicky. 'If a client's short, she shouldn't have masses of hair and needs volume on top, and someone very tall should steer clear of a close crop. But most people don't fall into either category and body shape is less important than what's fashionable at the time.' With one proviso. Always be aware of how your hair performs. If you have good thick locks, short styles will look great as well as long; but with thin or overly frizzy hair, some styles are impractical. The point being, don't necessarily try to copy a fashionable style; let the stylist adapt it to suit your hair.

Eliminating problems

Never let a problem go unconfronted: both dandruff and oily hair are unsightly, and usually unnecessary.

Dandruff sufferers: should rub a tiny amount of olive oil on the scalp between parted hair to soften the skin, and have a diet low in salt, high in light vegetable oils and low fat dairy produce. Wearing patterns, not plain dark colours, will make loose flakes less obvious until the problem is sorted out.

People with oily hair: must avoid fatty foods such as butter, cheese, bacon and full-fat milk, and can dab mild astringents on to the scalp such as a witch hazel, lemon and water blend.

Colouring hair

Over two years, top model Linda Evangelista had two radical hair colour changes: from her own brunette to peroxide blonde and then a Fifties fiery red. Likewise, Madonna dramatically altered her colouring to suit her mood. Each change by both women was right for the moment and all were deemed successes by press and public alike. But for most people violent, dense colour change doesn't work. 'Linda and Madonna are going for impact and have strong enough faces to carry it off,' warns Nicky Clarke. 'They also have good make-up artists standing by and the best photographers to make them look good. Without the right face and on older women, a solid wedge of colour can be dull, flat and frumpy.' *Long* densely dyed hair is a big mistake — it's very dated and has the texture of wire wool. In creating that Marilyn Monroe white blonde, remember that once bleach has been applied, your trials are only starting. The process is very drying and the hair's nearly at breaking point, so you can't blow-dry, use heated tongs, or go into the sun, and you must walk out of smoky atmospheres before your hair turns yellow. Moreover, you're never out of the hairdressers having the roots retouched. 'Most people should follow their skin tone and lighten their hair by only three or four shades,' Nicky believes. The streaks of highlighted hair that make your head look striped have fallen out of favour with colourist and client alike. The most natural highlights now are combined with darker tones to give the hair movement, provide depth and brighten and enrich the hair's own tones. The change is so subtle it lasts longer because grow-back is less obvious. However, because they're often faced with bleached highlights that have over-oxidised due to sun exposure and swimming in salt or chlorinated water, and that have lost their colour

Right *Hair can hold the balance of provocation with a mannish way of dressing. It's a potent juxtaposition fully exploited by silver screen stars like Marlene Dietrich and Lauren Bacall.*

balance and shine, some hairdressers are recommending their clients switch to tint, which is a combination of a milder bleach and conditioning colour. The bottom line is to check on a colourist's method—if he uses an old-fashioned rubber cap, run!

Dressing long hair

Long hair, worn loose and in immaculate condition, can be glorious straight. Three well-balanced meals a day with plenty of complex carbohydrate, a little protein and a small amount of fat is an important diet that will favour the growth of strong hair. But hair that's, say, twelve inches in length will be two years old, so how you treat it will determine its condition, and however heart-breaking, if the ends are split you should have them all lopped off. Mousse will add body and for maximum lift, hair can be raised vertically—not slightly forwards or back—and laid to dry over, not wrapped round, rollers at the roots. Gentle teasing widthways as well as on the crown, and smoothed over the top, pumps up the volume and suplies instant glamour. In curling long hair, you have to get the feeling right: watch what you wear - counteract any girliness inherent in long curly hair by wearing something strong and simple in cut. It's more fascinating and sexy, especially if you fake high gloss with a silicon serum—some of the best are by Wella and L'Oréal. Be careful about the type of curl you choose; unless they're natural, give permanent Bon Jovi corkscrew curls a wide berth—the flat table-top look when a perm grows out seems very amateurish. Chemicals have become so sophisticated that it's possible to make even the loosest of waves permanent. Perming just the ends on very big rollers provides a luxurious bounce, but a root perm to add lift is a bad investment, and grows out in less than a month. Also on the down side, it's a fallacy that perms mean less work because conditioning has to be so stringent; so resist the 'I'm going on holiday, must have a perm' syndrome—the first thing you'll do is go into the sun and turn your hair frizzy. Indeed, the weather plays an important part in maintaining a controlled appearance; it's pointless spending hours forming perfect curls if you know the minute you step outside, a drizzle will make them droop, or winds send them flying. On a good day, a head of big rollers with tighter pin curls at the front create temporary undulating waves, and will take up less time if put in when the hair is 80 per cent dry. Start by putting rollers in near the forehead and work back in a herringbone design, which steers clear of forming defined lines across the head. If you use pre-heated rollers, make sure the hair is cool before you remove them. Once they're out, you can either work

Left *Hair tied back opens up the nape and shoulders to be made a fuss of or left impressively bare.*

through the hair with your fingers to soften the curl, or concentrate each wave into glossy rolls with careful brushing. Curl lasts better in short hair because there's less weight to pull it out, but spraying each section of hair before rolling it up will improve the curl's durability. The easiest option is to put a few big rollers in the top layer of hair and add a few smaller ones at the end for bounce. Better still, take a tip from the models backstage at the collections and wrap your hair round Coca Cola cans!

Hair put up or tied back must be sophisticated or young and fresh, nothing in between. Never underestimate the appeal of the nape of the neck or a beautifully shaped head if the clothes and the occasion are right. Have plenty of pins at hand and get used to dealing with the back of the head, but go easy on elaborate hair ties and bows which can be too fussy. An elegant French pleat is easy to achieve with practice and less severe than a tight bun, a French plait or all-over braids. Don't wear upswept hair with a low-back dress unless you know your skin is in perfect condition. Hair doesn't have to be dragged tightly back from the face. Apart from breaking the hair shafts, over-zealous dragging can show unattractive strips of scalp. At the end of the summer, many women complain of hair loss round the forehead and it's usually because they scraped their hair back for coolness. Ponytails should be treated with extreme caution and must never be an excuse for forgetting about dirty hair. If the hair's over-layered, they're too scraggy; a blunt heavy flop looks best. And whilst a slide can create a fuller, fatter impression for thin hair tied back, it should be put in at the proper angle—preferably quite low so the hair is sleek and not stuck out a right angles like a jaunty schoolgirl. Neat elasticated tie-backs form a satisfying rounded drop or a quirky upright burst on top of the head. The latter can look great with sports wear, but wouldn't be taken seriously in business meetings. Be careful, too, as you get older: there tends to be a cut-off time for long hair worn loose; it can often drag down a more mature face. Young faces can afford to exaggerate a point with hair pieces and permanent extensions.

MAKE-UP

The trickle-down effect has had an enormous impact in the cosmetics industry over the last few years—subtle shades and protective ingredients, once only available in high-priced ranges, are now within reach of women on a budget and those who just want the freedom to experiment. Few women are truly selective at cosmetic counters and most buy irrational but expensive titbits to

HAIRCARE ESSENTIALS

Clean, glossy hair is pure pleasure, and to keep it sleek, without broken strands that spring sideways and deaden the sheen, a proper technique in shampooing, brushing and drying is imperative. Here's how.

Shampooing
• **Do** wet the hair well—that way you will be able to use less shampoo.

• **Don't** tip shampoo straight on to the hair; spread it over your palms to get overall coverage. Massage it in gently without using fingernails, and avoid adding more if there isn't much lather; some shampoos work better that way.

• **Don't** pile the hair on top of the head where it'll tangle; keep it hanging down.

• **Don't** wash your hair in the bath where you'll transfer dirty residues.

• **Do** forget dry shampoos that make the hair look dull.

• **Do** wash hair regularly: 'It's not true that washing is bad for your hair,' explains Glenn Lyons of the Philip Kingsley London Trichological Clinic.

'Once a day is beneficial, especially in the city, because it clears out pollution, and everybody should wash hair at least twice a week—sweat and oil can make the hair smell. One of the big dangers for hair is that it dries out; at least if you wet it you increase its moisture level.'

• **Do** rinse for ever. And rinse again.

Post-wash care
• **Don't** apply conditioner to the scalp, just the hair ends— you don't want its heaviness to detract from the hair's natural bounce. Conditioner eliminates tangles: combing through might tug and break hair without it.

• **Do** section the hair and work up from the bottom with a wide-toothed comb that has no seam down the teeth on which hair could catch, and preferably a rubber one to avoid the hair 'going electric'.

• **Don't** use brushes that have close bristles—they won't let the hair through, so the hair glosses over the top, or, worse, breaks.

• **Do** wash brushes and combs regularly in water to which a

teaspoon of bicarbonate of soda has been added. The dirt will immediately rise to the surface.

Drying and styling
Take one hair and measure it with a ruler. Healthy hair will stretch 25–35 per cent of its length before snapping. If the stretch is less, your hair is too dry. To keep the hair elastic:

• **Do** let the hair dry naturally as much as possible to avoid heat damage. If you use a dryer, direct the flow from root to end forcing the hair's cuticle to lie flat, and avoid the extra nozzles that concentrate the heat; keep the temperature low and disperse the flow.

• **Don't** overdo exposure to sun—especially coloured or permed hair—or the use of heated rollers. A little sun can brighten the hair and improve its thickness, but overexposure makes it brittle, coarse and spiky. The same goes for heated rollers and hot brushes, so try to make an unbiased judgment whether it might be better to sacrifice volume for condition.

GOOD TO THE LAST DROP

Treated sensibly, cosmetics will survive until they're finished. There are four straightforward laws:

• Always replace tops to jars straight after use to prevent dust, dirt and bacteria getting in, and to stem the destructive oxidation process. Tubes may last longer because they expose less of the contents to the elements.

• Keep cosmetics in a dark, cool place, even the fridge; heat and light may alter their properties.

• Fingers, brushes and sponges used to apply cosmetics must always be spotlessly clean to prevent contamination and clogging.

• If you tire of an item of make-up, don't throw it out: put it away for a while. In a few months, you can return to it and you'll be pleased to see it again.

cheer themselves up. Be sensible, not impulsive, about what you choose—where's the shopping logic if you have to buy a new sharpener to fit a new lip pencil?

A little make-up, well-applied, is infinitely preferable to a lot that draws attention from your overall appearance and natural expression. Make-up mustn't be treated as a mask to hide behind, but should add a new dimension to your clothes just like your hair. Experimental make-up is exhilarating and multiplies your looks to the power of X; think of the permutations in mixing a simple pair of jeans with natural/strong make-up and cowboy boots/pretty mules, for example. The ground rule is not to be too serious or sophisticated about it. 'The shape of your face doesn't matter for instance,' says top make-up artist Maggie Hunt. 'So long as you shade where you're plump and highlight the points you want to emphasise you don't have to be any more technical.' Ignore silly rules to make the eyes look closer or further apart, or that match make-up shades with the colour of your clothes or eyes. It's more modern to define your features subtlely, but be aware of fashion's nuances—is matt, a healthy sheen or gloss the order of the day? And pay attention to the *mood* of your clothes. For example, try countering the sweetness of pastels with berry or earth-coloured lipsticks; play a high-voltage cerise against an electric pink shirt; cool down bright print with naturals and let neutrals soften a stern navy work suit.

The beauty of make-up is its variety. Good make-up is altered minutely regularly and leaves people wondering what's different. A fresh youthful complexion with nothing more than a smidgen of mascara, blush and a flick of lip balm on lips has a brisk-walk effect and leaves room for, perhaps, accessory impact. Full make-up can look out of place, almost stuffy, in some situations, for example in the summer, on the beach, at the weekend or when playing sports. A natural make-up might be more appropriate in the countryside, at work, on days when you are wearing pale and understated clothes, or want to appear quietly confident, but is different from no make-up at all, and has to be superbly applied, which means well-blended colours that follow your hair colour and skin tone. Although it's difficult to generalise, for olive and light brown skins, terracotta, tawny browns, charcoal, salmon and fruit pinks look natural; for fair skins, pinky browns, ruddy browns, taupe, soft greys, and matt blush pinks are best; whereas dark skins can take blood reds, greys, pinky browns and berry shades. Where the natural look fails is when a woman changes to a hair colour that doesn't suit her skin tone. With dressed hair, in the evening, with clothes that say 'glamour', make-up can afford to be more radical, make greater use of liner pencils and go a colour further away from natural, though must never be crude. If you decide to pursue a fashion quirk, always be sure to know where the emphasis lies—if the eyebrows or lips become more pronounced, what also has changed to accommodate them?

Good make-up begins with a smooth, healthy skin; thereafter the choice is yours. It's worth deciding what to wear first, so you can adjust your make-up accordingly, and pull on any clothes that go over your head or you'll smudge everything. The light you work in is crucial and must be the same as the light for which your make-up is designed.

Foundation is meant to smooth out fluctuations in skin tone, and should mirror exactly your complexion. Make a distinction between the colour you wear in summer and the one you use in winter. Always test on your face—the skin on the back of your hand is different—and in daylight, not department store light. Technology in foundations has advanced into lighter mousses, subtle matt and light-diffusing effects, and moisturising and sunscreening formulations that allow for a natural light coverage, which are worth paying more for. Make sure you stroke foundation on in directions that follow any hair growth, right up to the eyes, including eyelids, but wipe it away from wrinkles where it will collect. Always hide spotty areas with foundation dotted on with a brush and beware of specially designed concealers that won't blend with your skin. Unless your body is more tanned than your face, or vice versa, it shouldn't be necessary to put foundation on your neck. Chances are, it will leave an unsightly tidemark inside a pristine shirt collar.

Powder should be dusted over foundation almost immediately to prevent the foundation from acting like a cleanser, most noticeably around the eyes where it can lift off mascara, leaving smears. There's no need to spend big amounts on powder, but it must be fine and either translucent or the same colour as your foundation. A compact makes sense for the handbag, but for setting foundation use loose, though a compact, knocked with a broad brush, will easily create loose powder.

Blusher should be similar to your natural colouring—tawny ones are usually more suited than fuchsias—and brushed on—not above or below—your cheekbones with a tapered brush that follows the contours of the face. Blusher can often double as eye shadow, lending a consistent look to the face. Cream blushers are harder to apply than powder ones and go on before face powder, unlike powder blushes which go on top. Avoid pearly blushers, which make cheeks stand out like Belisha beacons.

Eye shadows in matt shades, preferred by most professionals, used to be the province of only premium brands, but now less expensive lines are making them too. Don't apply pearl to the eyelids; apart from often being unfashionable, it tends to highlight crepy skin. Top make-up artists apply all powders with the applicator they're sold with, but then smooth and re-smooth with their own brushes to eliminate hard edges.

Mascara is a must for most women; those that have shied away from its theatricality, can now try the gels that have only a hint of colour. Your method of application of mascara will determine how natural your eyelashes look; a single quick flick just at the tips will be enough to define the lashes, but two coats swept on in directions towards the outer extreme of the eye create a more dramatic doe-eyed effect—though to prevent clogging you should always be sufficiently diligent to comb through thoroughly between coats. Moistened cake mascara painted over the base of the eyelashes will cover any light roots, and a black, dark brown or grey liquid liner or well-smoothed pencil will add depth to the lashes. A brighter liner draws attention to itself rather than to the subtle flow of colour from the lashes. If the top lid is large, the line can afford to go deeper; if the lid doesn't show, avoid a line altogether.

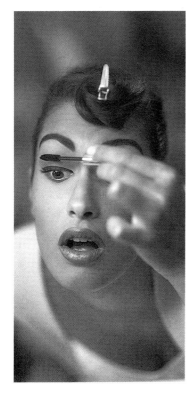

Above *Some mascaras promise to thicken lashes, but do so with filaments that initially stick to the ends only to fall off leaving telltale smudges. Reconcile yourself to your lashes' natural length and texture, and aim to darken them instead. That's what really gives the eye definition, and a no-mess alternative to mascara is having the lashed dyed professionally, an effect that lasts about six weeks. Using an eyelash curler 'opens' the eyes and helps disguise heavy eyelids.*

Eyebrow shape and thickness can be altered with pencils—whether Brooke Shields-bushy or slender and arched *à la* Marlene Dietrich, eyebrow shapes quickly go in and out of fashion – this way you do no permanent damage. Brush them clear of foundation downwards; then with a pencil swing the colour up to the highest point, and in a second movement go into a steady decline. Brush the hairs up again, over the pencil mark, but blunt the tops of the brow with your finger to stave off the werewolf look. Eye shadow or a pencil dabbed between the hairs, or stroking them with a nearly finished mascara wand, can subtly change the brows' colour and emphasise them more if you wish. A short cut to a neat shape without the fiddle of pencils is to brush through with a tiny amount of hair gel or clear eyelash gel. Then make a conscious effort to stop your hands rubbing them and putting you back to square one.

Left *If you define the lips, your whole face comes alive, but by the same token dark hairs above the top lip, stained teeth and cracked lips are also accentuated. Unconditioned lips are best kept natural.*

Lipsticks in matt generally last longest, then pearly and finally creamy ones. Cosmetic companies have been grappling with the problem of lipstick longevity for over half a century; a solution comes from Avon, with a lipstick which has micro-encapsulated pigment that is released every time you press your lips together. Slicking lipstick over foundation, using a lip brush—tapered but not too short, otherwise colour can't be painted on evenly—or laying a single tissue layer over newly painted lips, patting it with powder then reapplying are all techniques that foster staying power; with the latter, you'll lose any glossiness but that's easily remedied by a second, top coat or a dot of Vaseline in the centre of the bottom lip, which actually makes the lip look fuller. The best lipsticks are treatments too; the moisturising agents that started their career only at the top end of the market now are being incorporated by mass-market makes, though a keen investment if you regularly suffer from rough lips are Elizabeth Arden's Lip Spa lipsticks with vitamin E but which also include a new vital ingredient—water. Lip-liner pencils shouldn't be a corrective medium. What happens is liplines remain when the lipstick's rubbed off and you just look like you've missed your lips. They can disguise imperfections, and halt the bleeding of lipstick into creases, but an all-over stain effect created with pencils alone may be young and fresh. Always check whether you're paying more for a smudger or brush on the end of a pencil; they may be completely unnecessary, especially if you already have similar versions. Good pencils are neither too soft nor too hard and won't break when sharpening if they have a spell in the fridge

Above *Triumphal arches: drawing in brows calls for patience, practice and precision.*

TRAVELLING LIGHT

• In sunny climes, make-up may be less important than at home: it can melt and feel uncomfortable in extreme heat; a bare face with a warm glow may be more attractive, blotted with *papier poure* to play down shine; remember foundation used at home won't suit skin that's been in the sun.

• Limit the make-up you wear on a long flight; because the air in a plane is extremely dehydrating, you'll want to keep applying moisturiser, so it's best to avoid foundation. An Evian spray helps moisture loss and provides an instant freshen-up.

• Mascara that smudges is a pain when you're cat-napping on a long journey, so use a colourless gel or better still have your eyelashes dyed professionally beforehand.

• Take trial-size bottles, the ones that come free with bigger ones; or decant creams and cleansers into light and unbreakable plastic containers, but don't put them back into the originals on your return— you'll waste too much.

• Warm up the face with bronzing powder if you keep it but not the rest of your body tan-free.

• Always keep not-quite-finished and so lighter make-up for travelling and take a long fine brush to dig out last traces from elusive corners.

• Investigate multi-purpose cosmetics, such as the Body Shop's colour for eyes, cheeks and lips, and Colorfast's combination mascara and brow tamer that has three uses: lash primer, conditioning brow gel and mascara.

first. A broken lipstick can be repaired by carefully softening the broken ends over a candle flame and then pressing both ends firmly together—but wait till it cools before you use it. You don't need masses of different lipsticks; with just three, the mixes are infinite. In general, beware of pale pinks and frosted peaches, which make lips look narrow and too pretty by half, and, unless your features are strong or your skin lusciously dark, be wary of pillarbox reds, beside which the rest of your appearance fades.

Putting on the glitz
'If you've worn make-up all day and want to create an evening mood, it's better to retouch than to start again,' says Maggie Hunt. 'Freshen up your make-up with an Evian spray to dampen the foundation, making it easier to blend. Then if you need to add more, dot some on with a sponge, and powder afterwards. Wipe around your eyes with a dry cotton wool bud, especially in the crease lines—it's disastrous to moisten eye shadow. A charcoal matt eye shadow will define the outer corner of the eyes

more for evening, and whilst a soft grey or brown liner is best for day, liquid eye liner is more dramatic for night-time (but might be too strong for blondes). If you want to add more mascara, comb out what's already there first.' Evening is generally the environment in which to try out new make-up trends, but whilst the rule for after dark is that make-up can be heavier and glossier, never imagine that means glitter, frosting and gold! If you've applied your make-up properly, you shouldn't need to carry much in an evening bag, but powder, lip liner, a lipstick and cotton buds could be handy.

Below *Make-up on holiday should be kept to a minimum. Let nature have its way.*

Left *Altering your make-up is a way of moving from day to evening without changing your clothes: try defining brows and lips more, maybe warming pencils at the tip, which produces deeper, more lasting colour.*

SCENT

In Beverly Hills, as well as no-smoking areas, they now have scent-free zones. Take care you don't suffocate people with a powerful scent. You may have become immune to its strength; that mustn't mean you ladle on more. Try also to watch how many scents you mix—the moisturiser, soap, deodorant, shampoo and bath oil you use may all have a distinctive trait and shouldn't crash land on you; choose beauty products with very little perfume, or at least stick with one brand. On the flip side, one tip for smelling delicious all evening is to soak a little piece of cotton wool in something wonderful and slip it inside your bra. Unpleasant natural smells, such as body odour, sweaty feet and palms, are inexcusable: frequent washing, antiperspirants and controlling nervous tension—avoid coffee, tea and soft drinks that contain caffeine—can keep these at bay. Leather-soled shoes, cotton—not wool or synthetic—socks let feet breathe.

Right *To hurry in such quiet, classic clothes would do them an injustice.*

POSTURE

Deportment is an antiquated word that brings to mind prissy girls with no better purpose than to glide about with books on their heads, but an ugly, feet-splayed lollop or a slovenly slouch in a chair pays the very best of clothes no favours. Rather than being stuffy, good posture is elegant. *Vogue*'s delicious explanation in the Twenties of the principles of good posture as 'an utter lack of rigidity, an appearance of having been dropped into one's clothes and remaining there by accident' still pinpoints the spirit. No silliness there, just a sense of charm. The rules are simple: pull yourself out of your hips, as if a thread attached to your head is drawing you up and up, your stomach in, pelvis tucked under, chin up, and neck and shoulders back but relaxed; standing sideways in a mirror, an imaginary plumbline from shoulder to ankle should cut through your hip and knees. Now face the mirror and check that you are standing symmetrically, not with one shoulder higher or a hip stuck out. An effortless, correct stance is a boost to your bearing, and a jacket or a pair of trousers can hang properly without any extra folds and stress points.

How you move, your every gesture, is part of your character and really shouldn't be overly tampered with, but make exceptions so you do your clothes justice. Before sitting, pick up the habit of first pulling trousers up around the knees to prevent bagginess—as men do—and tucking under skirts and coats, maybe even hanging up a jacket. And don't flop heavily on to a seat, but meet it with control! Also try to make walking in high heels look easy, or accept that low heels bring out your better movements. On days that you know you'll be rushing, again, wear a low shoe. Likewise, when getting out of cars and deep squashy sofas, when sitting on tall stools and climbing big steps, short skirts may make you move self-consciously and trousers are a more flattering choice. You should treat your movements like accessories and let the day decide whether you wear them.

LOOKING LIVELY

Being fit feels wonderful. Fitness that comes from regular exercise stimulates the mind, awakes the senses and untaps reserves of energy you never knew you had. It's one of the best beauty products to invest in. Quite apart from the benefits to body shape, exercise puts a spring in the step, makes you aware of your posture and you look alert. It boosts the circulation, which brings blood to the face and takes toxins away. The result? A fresher skin. Simple. Your health improves—exercise definitely eases stress-related illnesses and recent research suggests could charge the body's batteries against minor irritations like colds.

Undoubtedly, a toned, slim body increases the number of styles you can wear. Tight leggings and cropped jackets are not a look for flabby thighs, for example; flat pumps make fat calves look even chunkier and short-sleeved summer dresses don't work with chubby arms. Good muscle tone is sexy; it's a pleasure to show off a shapely leg or a tight waist, and to be able to waiver between skinnyribs and baggy sweaters. Try to be realistic, though. Your genes, not exercise, dictate whether or not you're tall, broad or long-legged, and provided you're fit, whatever shape you are, all's well. For anyone who doesn't exercise, the body's main source of energy is carbohydrate: the fat won't budge. But a balanced low-fat diet and moderate regular exercise, which burns up excess fat, will optimise your shape. If you do diet, be careful not to lose muscle. Clothes don't hang properly on a bag of bones, so it's wise to coincide a diet with some form of resistance training. Although resistance machines and weights are largely the domain of expensive gyms and health clubs, instructive videos, ankle weights and dumbells are reasonably priced and can be used in the privacy of your home.

Physical fitness is a broad term. The way a hammer thrower sees fitness, for example, will be very different from the needs of a gymnast, or yours for that matter. The aim is to find a level that's right for you. Excessive, obsessive exercise may be wholly unnecessary for day-to-day life and you shouldn't underestimate the benefits in a brisk walk to work, in bounding up stairs and spurning lifts, in hoovering with a will. For great body shape, the American College of Sports Medicine recommends everyone should get some form of aerobic exercise between three and five times a week, for a minimum of twenty minutes—any less and it's difficult to lose weight. If you have a choice between a long low-intensity programme and a short but high intensity one, go for the former: workouts of high intensity may include high-impact movements and you run a greater risk of injury. During a safe workout it should be possible to have a normal conversation.

Always choose an activity you enjoy; that way you're more likely to stick at it. Vary what you do; substitute a run with an hour of tennis. The change will improve your flexibility. If you think about taking classes at a fitness centre, check the teachers' qualifications; a badly taught class is less than useless. You can save on exercise clothes; so long as they're comfortable, retain heat and absorb sweat, that's fine. Spend more on your shoes.

Below *To look great you have to feel great.*

WELL-BEING

Stress shows. Quite aside from the havoc it wreaks on our internal mechanism and our concentration, frown lines, an insincere smile, a drained face, a twitch, spots, bitten nails, rashes, droopy hair, jerky movements and irritability are all unappealing, visible symptoms of being uptight. If the body's tense and awkward, wonderful clothes are an unconvincing veneer. Relaxation is an important contributor to looking great: 'If you do yoga ... you can postpone facelifts for years,' reported American *Vogue* in the early Nineties. Nature intended man to rest: his heart actually rests longer than it works—for every 0.3 seconds of its muscle activity, there is a rest period of 0.5 seconds; and even during labour, between contractions, the uterus pauses at length to build up to the final delivery. Some cultures have taken the hint and work reflective parts of the day into daily life—the Chinese have T'ai Chi, the Mediterraneans their siesta, the French take long lunches and the people of India meditate—but British tradition says plough on till bedtime. Yet putting aside time to pay yourself attention recharges the batteries and puts anxieties in perspective—a big problem becomes a worry becomes a minor irritation, and stress's physical ravages find it harder to take hold.

To maintain a calm, controlled exterior, how we perform daily tasks has to be monitored. Pay attention to the way you hold a phone, for example. Is it with a white-knuckle or an easy grip? Do you sit rigid on the bus? Are the muscles of your face relaxed as you walk along the street? Always make time to take lunch away from work, with friends if possible, and don't rush your food, make meals a time of relaxation. Try not to book up your diary so you're frantically busy every evening. Make sleep a priority and have the courage to say no if friends want you to go out, so you're at your best when you do say yes. Relaxation is not a state of physical collapse, sinking in front of the TV; it's the time the body switches off. Here are ten ways how:

1. Lie on the floor in a warm, quiet room, with a pillow under your head, your arms resting on your stomach. Gently elongate your muscles and open up your joints zone by zone. Slowly pull your shoulders down as far as they'll go and then stop. Push your elbows out away from your body without moving the position of your hands and stop. Lengthen your hands. Turn your hips outwards and push your feet away from your body. Press your body and head into the floor and pillow, transferring all your weight on to the supports. Your body will feel longer, almost liberated.

DAMSELS IN DE-STRESS

Lisa Bruce, Designer: 'I relax by taking my imaginary dog, Walter, for a walk, by stroking and fondling my Manolo Blahnik shoes, by lying in the summer's longest grass and exercising my senses.'

Darcey Bussell, Dancer with the Royal Ballet, Covent Garden: 'I convince myself I'm not stressed, especially before a performance.'

Bella Freud, Designer: 'Exercise gets rid of my freaked-out feelings; otherwise, sitting by a fire, watching the ice-skating on TV.'

Nicole Farhi, Designer: 'I sculpt in a conservatory at the back of my house, where I can't hear the phone.'

Polly Sellar, Beauty Editor, British *Vogue*: 'I rollerblade in the park, sail and work out in the gym. My natural instinct is to do nothing, but I know relaxation from activity is much more profound; if I'm physically exhausted my mind relaxes and I sleep well.'

Edina Ronay, Designer: 'I practise the Alexander Technique, and watch three old films a week.'

2. Lie on the floor and, instead of stretching, consciously relax each minute part of your body in turn, starting from the toes
and working up: think about your ankles, calves, knees, thighs,
hips, stomach, moving through the arms, neck, face and skull.
When you get to the face, relax your jaw, mouth, tongue, cheeks,
eyes, eyebrow area, temple and scalp. This is a wonderful,
speedy pick-me-up that takes just five minutes, so you can make
a point of doing it every day.

3. Concentrate on areas that feel particularly tense. Use your
three middle fingers to press below the bones behind your ears
and slide up and down a tight neck. A taut muscle along
shoulders and top of the back can be kneaded with slow pinching
movements. To self-massage the back, place a tennis ball between you and a wall and, bending your knees to move it up and
down, gently work on areas of tension with the ball. A rolling pin
stroked up and down thighs also smooths away tension.

4. Have an evening without television.

5. Make bathtime a luxury. Take the phone off the hook,
warm up your bathrobe and towels and add something wonderfully scented to the water. Maybe sprinkle in a few petals, play
classical music if you're in the mood, and dim the light. Slowly
sway in the water, shut your eyes and open the mind.

6. Spend a whole evening winding down and preparing for
bedtime. Float round in a dressing-gown, play music you love
(dancing if you like). Warm up your bed, put flowers in your
room and light scented candles, so your bedroom seems peaceful
and protective. Avoid tea and coffee, prepare a light healthy
meal, and treat yourself to a pampering session: a pedicure and
manicure, a hot oil treatment for your hair, a home facial.

7. With practice, DIY aromatherapy can be supremely relaxing. Essential oils are massaged into the skin—the face, back,
chest, top of the hands, soles of the feet—or are added to warm
water or inhaled, but you need to be knowledgeable about the
oils and their effects. Always do a patch test on your skin before
using an oil for the first time. If you add a few drops to bath
water, mix them with a tiny bit of shampoo first so the drops disperse. The Natural by Nature Oils Aromatherapy Centre recommends using seven drops per bath, perhaps lavender and frankin-
cense for a relaxing experience, geranium for something more
uplifting, ylang-ylang for a sweet, exotic sedative, marjoram for
freshness. If you massage in the oils, you'll have to dilute them in
sweet almond oil or grape seed oil by 98 per cent, that is, to 50
millilitres of vegetable oil add twenty-five drops. To make massage less of a stupifier, mix in a fruit oil, for example mandarin.

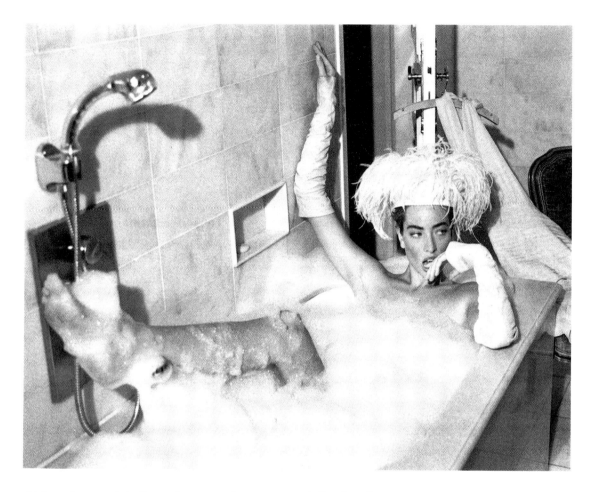

Although essential oils can be expensive, try a specialist shop for a wide range and instructions, or ready-mixed concoctions from recognised aromatherapists.

Above *A little of what you fancy does you good.*

8. Invest in a professional treatment: reflexology, which eases away tensions by massaging nerve endings in your feet; an hour's flotation in a strong solution of Epsom salts in a warm, dark, quiet tank—no, it's not claustrophobic! A facial; a sauna; a blow-dry: anywhere you get personal attention.

9. Learn to meditate or practise yoga. There are many books and videos that show you how.

10. Have a change of scene—anything that takes you away from your routine helps dissolve tension. Book in a weekend stay with friends or family; you don't need to go far to pick up a new perspective. Read up about a subject you're interested in, really become an authority. Take up a hobby that provides a fresh group of friends with a common interest, or join a cheap evening class that sometimes has trips away at the weekend.